Byron

SUTTON POCKET BIOGRAPHIES

Series Editor C.S. Nicholls

Highly readable brief lives of those who have played a significant part in history, and whose contributions still influence contemporary culture.

SUTTON POCKET BIOGRAPHIES

Byron

CATHERINE PETERS

SUTTON PUBLISHING

First published in 2000 by
Sutton Publishing Limited · Phoenix Mill
Thrupp · Stroud · Gloucestershire · GL5 2BU

British Library Cataloguing in Publication Data

A catalogue record for this book is available from the British
Library

ISBN 0-7509-2124-2

Typeset in 13/18 pt Perpetua.
Typesetting and origination by
Sutton Publishing Limited.
Printed in Great Britain by
Cox & Wyman, Reading, Berkshire.

CONTENTS

CHRONOLOGY

1788	**22 January**. George Gordon Byron born London.
1788/9	Taken by mother to Aberdeen.
1791	**2 August**. Father dies.
1794–8	At Aberdeen Grammar School.
1798	**21 May**. Byron becomes 6th Baron Byron of Rochdale.
	August. He goes to Newstead Abbey with mother.
1799	**September**. Enters Dr Glennie's school, Dulwich.
1801	**April**. Enters Harrow School.
1805	**October**. Enters Trinity College, Cambridge.
1805–6	**December–April and October–December**. Absent from Cambridge.
1806	**November**. First collection of poems, *Fugitive Pieces*, privately printed.
1807	**January**. *Poems on Various Occasions* published.
1808	**September**. Takes possession of Newstead Abbey.
1809	**22 January**. Comes of age.
	1 March. *English Bards and Scotch Reviewers* published.
	13 March. Takes his seat in the House of Lords.
	2 July. Leaves England.

Chronology

1809–11	Travelling in Europe, Greece and Turkey.
1811	**8 July**. Returns to England.
	1 August. Mrs Byron dies.
1812	**27 February**. Makes maiden speech in House of Lords.
	10 March. Publication of *Childe Harold* Cantos I and II make Byron famous. Affairs with Lady Caroline Lamb and Lady Oxford.
1813–14	Affair with his half-sister Augusta Leigh.
	15 September. Becomes engaged to Annabella Milbanke.
1815	**2 January**. Marries Annabella Milbanke.
	10 December. Daughter, Augusta Ada Byron, born.
1816	**15 January**. Lady Byron returns to her parents' house.
	21 April. Deed of Separation signed.
	25 April. Byron leaves England.
	May–October. Living in Switzerland. Becomes friendly with Shelley. Claire Clairmont becomes pregnant by Byron.
	November. Settles in Venice, his home for the next three years.
1817	**12 January**. Birth of Allegra, Byron's daughter by Claire Clairmont.
	10 December. Hears that Newstead Abbey has been sold.
1818	**28 February**. *Beppo* published.
	May. Takes charge of his daughter Allegra.
	3 July. Begins *Don Juan*.

Chronology

1819   **April**. Begins affair with Countess Teresa Guiccioli.

1820   Living in Ravenna.

July. Countess Guiccioli granted separation from her husband. Byron joins Carbonari, an Italian revolutionary society.

1821   **1 March**. Places Allegra in convent at Bagnacavallo.

November. Moves to Pisa, where Shelley is living.

1822   **20 April**. Allegra dies of typhoid fever.

8 July. Shelley drowns.

September. Moves to Genoa. Involved with Leigh Hunt in publication of the *Liberal*.

1823   **June**. Makes plans to leave for Greece to join in the struggle to overthrow Turkish rule.

3 August. Arrives Cephalonia.

1824   **5 January**. Arrives Missolonghi.

15 February. Has severe convulsions, similar to epileptic fit.

9 April. After riding in the rain becomes seriously ill.

19 April. Dies.

INTRODUCTION

But words are things, and a small drop of ink,
Falling like dew upon a thought, produces
That which makes thousands, perhaps millions, think.[1]

On a May morning in 1824, six men gathered in the elegant drawing-room of the publisher John Murray's premises in Albemarle Street. Before them on the table lay Byron's manuscript memoirs, given to Thomas Moore to publish posthumously. The news of Byron's death in Greece, a month earlier, had only just reached London.

Four of those present had not read the memoirs, but nevertheless argued vehemently that they should be destroyed. Two were representing Byron's estranged wife and his sister, both with reasons to oppose publication. More surprisingly, Byron's oldest friend John Cam Hobhouse and his publisher John Murray also voted for destruction, to protect Byron's reputation: 'such regard have I', said Murray, 'for Lord Byron's fame and honour'.[2]

Moore, who had read the book, vehemently objected to having the work condemned unread 'as if it were a pest bag'[3] but was finally overruled. Murray's sixteen-year-old son was brought into the room to witness the historic moment, as the manuscript and the only copy were solemnly torn up and fed into the fire.

By an irony that Byron would have appreciated, the burning of the memoirs only perpetuated the rumours of black deeds and nameless horrors, though Byron had been careful to avoid anything that would harm the living, and described the first part of the memoirs as *Hamlet* without the Prince. He had already been refused burial in Westminster Abbey. In the 1830s a statue of him intended for the Abbey was rejected. It almost went to the Louvre, before a home was found for it in the Wren Library at Trinity College, Cambridge. Not until 1969 was a memorial to one of the great Romantic poets unveiled in Poets' Corner in Westminster Abbey. The English establishment tried, without success, to obliterate Byron from public memory.

The truth about Byron's life has been painstakingly reconstructed in the past half-century, from his letters and journals and from the private papers of others. Yet, for all the millions of words that have been written about him, Byron remains an enigma. Apparently the most revelatory of writers, he is so variable, so self-contradictory, that it is impossible to know which confession is true, which avowal sincere, which love the crucial and defining emotion. Byron said of himself that he was only consistent in his political opinions. Biographers differ fundamentally on the interpretation of his character, his psychological state, his physical illnesses. The main orientation of his sexuality remains in doubt. It sometimes seems that there are as many Byrons as there are biographies of him.

What is not in doubt is Byron's poetic genius. Though critical opinion has shifted away from universal admiration of *Childe Harold* and his Eastern tales, once best-sellers on an unprecedented scale, *Don Juan*, attacked in his own day for immorality and cynicism, has now been recognized as the great comic and satiric epic of the Romantic era. Byron's prose is also outstanding. His letters and diaries are perceptive, original, witty and outrageously entertaining.

We shall never know the whole truth about him, but his work was, as Byron himself realized, intimately bound up with his life. Though his writing is great enough to stand alone, even a brief outline of his life can help to illuminate aspects of his subtle and complex poetry.

An Orphan of the Heart, 1788–1805

Few are my years, and yet I feel
The World was ne'er designed for me:[1]

When George Gordon Byron was born on 22 January 1788 the cards seemed stacked against him. The child of warring parents in deep financial trouble, from families notorious for instability and violence, he was also born with a malformed right leg and foot. No one could have predicted the meteoric blaze of his brief career as the famous (and infamous) Lord Byron, a romantic legend in his own lifetime. His lasting reputation as one of England's major poets would have seemed equally unlikely.

His 24-year-old mother, Catherine Gordon Byron, was the second wife, and hapless victim, of

Captain 'Mad Jack' Byron. When her only child was born she was living alone in modest lodgings off London's Oxford Street. Captain Byron was in hiding from his creditors. He came from an ancient and aristocratic family, but he was an incorrigible spendthrift, gambler and womaniser. He had earlier run away with Lady Carmarthen, a married woman who was an heiress in her own right, and married her after a scandalous divorce. When she died in 1784 leaving him with one surviving daughter of the marriage, Augusta, her income died with her. The Captain had already run through her other assets. At Bath, a popular spot with fortune-hunters, he soon marked down another victim, the awkward, noisy, overweight Catherine Gordon, a Scottish girl with a fortune of £25,000.

Catherine was also from an ancient family and, like the Byrons, the Gordons of Gight were known for their violent behaviour. Both Catherine's father and grandfather had drowned themselves. Catherine herself was given to emotional excesses, swinging between extravagant demonstrativeness and violent rage. She was not unintelligent, but superstitious and poorly educated. Her husband soon claimed she was impossible to live with, and her son later agreed.

Captain Byron must have had the charm his son inherited, for Catherine was besotted with him. She insisted on marrying him, against her family's wishes. There was no marriage settlement, and by the time their only child was born three years later, she was begging the lawyers to put the little money she had left in trust, lest it be wheedled out of her by her husband.

Catherine had the boy christened with the names of her own father, and retreated to Scotland where she brought him up, economically but respectably, in a rented apartment in Aberdeen. When her husband followed, they quarrelled incessantly. Byron claimed to remember the rows, and said they gave him a horror of matrimony. Captain Byron first retreated to lodgings on his own, then disappeared to France to live with his sister; it has been suggested that they had an incestuous relationship. He took no interest in his son, stating flatly that it was impossible he would ever walk, and never saw the boy again. In the summer of 1791 he died in Valenciennes, possibly by his own hand, so destitute that he did not have a coat to go out in. When Catherine Byron heard the news, her screams could, it was reported, be heard throughout the street.

In spite of her erratic behaviour, Catherine was a devoted mother, determined that her crippled son should receive treatment, learn to walk and have the best education she could afford. At three, when other children were running freely, he still had to be carried everywhere. But by four he was walking, and later had a pony to take him longer distances. He developed a distinctive gliding walk to hide his lameness, and learned to swim, a sport that became a life-long passion.

Byron was remembered in Scotland as a tempestuous, wilful child. The clash of temperaments with his equally difficult mother made for an uneasy household. Catherine would indulge him and overwhelm him with demonstrative affection, then scream that he was a lame brat, a typical Byron like his father. Byron's life-long sensitivity about his disability, which his friends thought morbid, began with her taunts, and he never forgave her for them. In the last year of his life he wrote a play, *The Deformed Transformed*, which opens with a mother attacking her crippled son for being 'a monstrous sport of nature'.[2] In *Don Juan* Byron declared that children deprived of parental tenderness were 'orphans of the heart'.[3]

Yet his mother had virtues that were to be of service to him. A passionate Whig, interested in contemporary affairs, she had a permanent effect on her son's political views. She was also a good manager, thrifty with her small remaining income, denying herself but unfailingly generous to her spendthrift son.

Byron was almost five when he went to a small school where, he said, he learned nothing, and then went to the grammar school at six. He was taken to church every Sunday, and the gloomy Calvinist creed of predestination was reinforced at home by Bible readings with their servant. He came to think of his disability as a punishment from God for some unknown sin.

Occasionally the grey streets of Aberdeen were exchanged for the Scottish Highlands on visits to the grandmother, Margaret Duff, who had brought up Byron's mother. Here he fell in love with the romantic landscape, and also with his cousin Mary Duff. He wrote later of his precocious emotion: 'How very odd that I should have been so utterly, devotedly fond of that girl. I certainly had no sexual ideas for years afterwards; and yet my misery, my love for that girl were so violent, that I sometimes doubt if I have ever been really attached since.'[4]

In 1794, Byron's cousin, the grandson and heir of the 5th Lord Byron, unexpectedly died. Byron became the heir of his great-uncle William, the 'wicked Lord Byron', perhaps the worst of that unstable family. Arraigned for murder when he killed his neighbour and cousin, William Chaworth, in a dubious duel in a dark room, he was convicted by his peers of the lesser charge of manslaughter. Ostracized by London society, he retreated to his estate of Newstead Abbey, near Nottingham, where he built a folly rumoured to be the scene of obscene orgies, and conducted mock naval battles (with real ammunition) on the lake. His mental and physical cruelty to his wife was so extreme that she eventually left him. He broke off relations with his son, quarrelled with his neighbours and conducted an open affair with a servant. He took no interest in his new heir and refused to provide any support for him. Instead he devastated the estate, cutting down the ancient trees and slaughtering the deer in the park. On his death in 1798, the ten-year-old Byron became the 6th Baron Byron of Rochdale.

As soon as Mrs Byron could arrange her affairs and sell her furniture to raise a little cash, they set off for Newstead. Byron's life changed dramatically. The little cripple with a broad Scots accent, living in obscure poverty, suddenly found himself a lord, owner of a notable, though dilapidated, property and potentially valuable estates. The ancient house, vividly described as 'Norman Abbey' in Canto XIII of *Don Juan*, had been built around the ruins of a still more ancient Cistercian abbey. Hidden in a wooded valley with a lake before it, Newstead is the most appropriate place imaginable for the nurturing of a poetic mind.

Byron's mother, however, faced practical problems. The old lord's creditors had seized most of the furniture; the neglected, partly roofless house needed expensive repairs to make it habitable; the park needed to be replanted with trees and restocked with game; the estate was producing almost no revenues. After essential repairs, the house would be let, for they could not afford to live there. For the time being they camped out in the rambling mansion, and Byron wandered through the empty rooms and devastated grounds, his imagination kindled by everything around him. He planted an oak sapling near the house, an earnest of regeneration.

After a few months Byron was sent to lodgings in Nottingham, for treatment by a self-styled surgeon, a quack who tried to stretch his leg and straighten his foot in a contraption that did no good and caused the boy great pain. He bore it stoically, but the damage was compounded by the behaviour of his nurse May Gray, who accompanied him. She was a Calvinist Scot who indoctrinated him with the terrifying creed of predestination at one moment, neglected him while she entertained men at others, and frequently beat him, she also, Byron revealed to his solicitor John Hanson, subjected him to sexual abuse. Byron himself attributed the peculiarities of his sexual temperament to these experiences.

At Hanson's insistence, the boy was separated from his nurse and taken to London, where more expert medical advice was sought from Matthew Baillie, a leading physician who treated the royal family, and the famous surgeon John Hunter, who had seen Byron when he was born. A brace was made, which Byron hated and wore as little as possible. Later he was to wear a special shoe, cosmetic rather than remedial, inside a normal boot.

Hanson had persuaded Byron's distant relative, the Earl of Carlisle, to become the boy's guardian,

but the practical arrangements were all decided by
Hanson himself who, for the only time in his long
association with Byron, showed judgement and
energy. The boy was sent to a small school in
Dulwich in the autumn of 1799, to prepare him for
a public school. Though he was eager to learn, and
clever, he found himself humiliatingly backward
compared with other boys of his age. He was also
increasingly embarrassed by his corpulent, ebullient
mother, who argued loudly with the headmaster
when she was not allowed to take her son out
during school hours. 'Byron, your mother is a fool',
one of his companions told him. 'I know it', he
replied, with shame.[5]

At thirteen Byron went to Harrow, where
Hanson's son was a pupil. The Byron family tradition
was for sons to be educated at Eton, though the
poet's father had been to Westminster. However, the
Harrow regime was more kindly, and less demanding
academically. Nevertheless, at first he hated it. The
school's position on a hill was a problem for a boy
who found walking difficult. Mrs Drury, the
headmaster's wife, remembered him 'straggling up
the Hill like a ship in a storm without a rudder or
compass'.[6] Swimming was a sport at which he could

compete on equal terms, but the bathing place was 2 miles from the school, and he had to hire a pony to get there: one of the masters then accused him of unnecessary extravagance. The legendary beauty that made him irresistible to both men and women came later: he was a fat boy, and a contemporary recalled him as being a most unromantic figure, 'with an iron-cramp on one of his feet, with loose corduroy trousers plentifully relieved by ink, and with fingernails bitten to the quick'.[7] Byron was teased about his disability, and would sometimes wake to find his foot in a bucket of water.

Byron did not try to ingratiate himself. Napoleon was already his hero, and when war against the French broke out again in 1803 he fought valiantly to defend a bust he owned of the Emperor, who was generally regarded in England as a monster. Byron had great physical courage, and fought his way to respect, often in defence of younger boys, but he was shy and lonely. He liked to lie by himself on a gravestone in the churchyard next to the school, dreaming or reading voraciously, absorbing literature and history rather than the classics he should have been studying. He infuriated his teachers, who found him arrogant and a bad influence. His letters home are full of complaints about their unfairness, but his headmaster treated him leniently. Byron was twice allowed to return to school after long unauthorized absences, the first time after a disagreement with his schoolmaster, only resolved when he was placed in the care of a different teacher.

On the second occasion, he was in love. The fifteen-year-old Byron refused to go back for the autumn term of 1803 and skulked at Newstead, now let to a Lord Grey, adamant that he would neither go to Harrow nor to his mother, living in a rented house nearby at Southwell. He had become obsessed with his distant cousin, Mary Chaworth. Mary, related to the man assassinated by the 'Wicked Lord', was already eighteen and soon to be married. Her family home, Annesley Hall, was a short distance from Newstead. Byron spent most of the summer haunting Annesley, and only gave in and returned to Harrow at the end of January 1804 when he overheard her say to her maid, 'What! Me care for that lame boy!' For years he continued to think that it was the great disaster of his life that he had not married Mary Chaworth.

Byron's friend and biographer Thomas Moore perceptively wrote of his 'disposition . . . to form strong attachments, and a yearning desire after affection in return, [which] were the feeling and the want that formed the dream and torment of his existence'.[8] His friendships, the love affairs that occupied much of his time from early adolescence, even his strong feeling for animals, especially dogs, were all expressions of this need. By 1806 he had two dogs: Boatswain was a gentle Newfoundland, Nelson a bulldog who was so ferocious that he later had to be destroyed. He also had two horses, Brighton and Sultan. They were the foundation of a growing menagerie; for the rest of his life Byron always had animals around him.

Byron's love affairs, though they tended to be brief, were deeply felt, and often painful. Acutely conscious of his physical defect, and unable to shake off the fear of predestined damnation inculcated by May Gray, he found it difficult to believe that anyone could love him. His feeling for Mary Duff remained strong enough to make him burst into tears when he heard of her marriage, when he was sixteen. A more ephemeral fancy for Margaret Parker, yet another cousin, who died young, led to his 'first dash into poetry'.[9] His friendships in boyhood also had the passionate intensity of love, and in his last two years at Harrow this craving for reassurance was expressed in attachments to several of the younger boys. Whether these were more than emotional friendships is impossible to establish. Homosexuality was widespread in English public schools, and Byron's Cambridge friend John Cam Hobhouse said that Byron 'had nothing to learn in the way of depravity either of mind or body when he came from Harrow'.[10] Yet Byron was disgusted when Lord Grey, the young man who had rented Newstead Abbey, made a homosexual advance – at the time Byron was obsessed with Mary Chaworth. The event caused him to break off his friendship with Lord Grey. He refused to explain himself to his mother, and still referred to the episode with distaste several years later.

Byron's last year and a half at Harrow were happy, and he wrote feelingly of 'Friendship, the dear peculiar bond of youth' in a poem of 1807.[11] He had a widening circle of friends. Under the influence of the headmaster, Joseph Drury, who had a passion for English poetry, he discovered the work of Alexander Pope and other eighteenth-century writers, and began to write verse himself. He took part in school plays, enjoying ranting as King Lear, and even (with a runner) played in the first Eton and Harrow cricket match. A change of headmaster elicited his first satire, and throughout his career he was to write both lyrical and satirical verse.

Life at home was not so satisfactory. In 'Childish Recollections', the 1807 poem quoted above, Byron wrote bitterly,

> friendship will be doubly dear
> To one, who thus for kindred hearts must roam
> And seek abroad, the love denied at home.

His relationship with his mother deteriorated to breaking point. As he clashed with her, he came to romanticize his dead father, and by extension, came to see his half-sister Augusta as 'a relation whom I love, a Friend in whom I can confide'.[12] He turned to her for the motherly affection he craved, venting his misery in outspoken letters.

Though they met at least once while he was at Dulwich, until 1804 Augusta, three and a half years older than Byron, had played little part in his life. She had been brought up by her maternal relatives, who did not encourage her to have anything to do with her disgraceful father's family. However,

Augusta, herself painfully shy, knew the difficulties of being an orphan, and became concerned for the proud, self-conscious boy.

Byron gave Augusta vivid accounts of his mother's abuse. She attacked his father, telling the boy he took after him. He admitted his mother's generosity and real affection for him, 'But her conduct is so strange, her caprices so impossible to be complied with, her passions so outrageous, that the evil quite overbalances her *agreeable qualities*.'[13] Six months later he had decided his mother was mad.

Augusta had problems of her own. She was in love with her cousin George Leigh, the son of her father's sister Frances. The frequent marriages between cousins in the Byron family undoubtedly reinforced the psychological instability that can be traced down the generations, and her mother's relations all disapproved. Captain Leigh had most of the Byron vices and was a compulsive gambler, in constant financial difficulties. He was also a bore, interested only in horses. But Augusta was determined. 'She married a fool – but she *would* have him'[14] was Byron's later verdict. They were eventually married in 1807.

By then Byron was at Cambridge. He was reluctant to leave Harrow, and most of his school friends were going to Oxford. There was no vacancy at Christ Church, however, and he went up to Trinity College, Cambridge, in October 1805, aged seventeen and a half. 'It was one of the deadliest and heaviest feelings of my life to feel I was no longer a boy', he remembered. 'From that moment I began to grow old in my own esteem.'[15]

YOUTH, 1807–9

In my hot youth, when George the Third was King[1]

Mrs Byron wrung a generous allowance of £500 a year from her son's trustees, hoping to keep him clear of debt at Cambridge. She was soon disillusioned. While she pinched and saved, Byron decorated and furnished his rooms in Trinity Great Court lavishly, kept a servant (who cheated him) and a horse. He treated the university as if it existed for his convenience. His Cambridge tutor was as perplexed by him as his schoolmasters had been.

As a nobleman Byron could graduate without taking an exam, simply by spending three years at the university. He seems never to have attended a lecture or written an essay, though he insisted he was not only idling and carousing, but reading widely. Certainly he was writing verse. A satire criticizing the narrow syllabus and the self-

satisfied dons, written and published in 1806, did
nothing to endear him to the authorities. He
spent so little of his three years actually in
residence that he was eventually only granted his
nominal degree after some delay and then very
reluctantly. Nevertheless, it was a crucial period
in his life.

In his first term Byron fell passionately in love
with a fifteen-year-old choirboy, John Edleston.
Byron was overwhelmed by his feelings, which
he later described as 'a violent, though *pure*, love
and passion'.[2] For the first time in his life he
believed he was truly loved in return. Physical
expression was limited to passionate kisses and
embraces, but Byron hatched romantic,
unrealistic plans to retire from the world as soon
as he was of age and live with Edleston at
Newstead.

By the end of his first term Byron was heavily in
debt. He spent the Christmas vacation in London,
trying urgently to raise a loan and being introduced
to the money-lenders who were to be his financial
undoing. Separation, Byron more than once
admitted, was usually a cure for his infatuations, and
he showed no anxiety to be reunited with Edleston.

Instead he lingered, mixing mostly with raffish underworld companions, until the middle of April 1806. Admonished for his unauthorized absence from Cambridge, he retorted that the university had nothing to offer him, and he was thinking of going abroad with a tutor. He rapidly returned when he discovered that his allowance would be discontinued if he left Cambridge. But by the summer his mounting debts meant he could no longer get credit from the Cambridge tradesmen, and he retreated to Southwell.

In spite of continued conflict with his mother, Byron remained there for most of the next year. He suffered periods of severe depression, to recur throughout his life, from which he sought relief in writing. 'To withdraw *myself* from *myself* . . . has ever been my sole, my entire, my sincere motive in scribbling at all', he declared six years later.[3]

He also occupied himself with the local girls. One entanglement almost led to a duel, when her family tried to entrap him into marriage. Another inspired a sexually explicit poem which caused a scandal when it was included in his first collection of verse, *Fugitive Pieces*. Byron swiftly recalled the privately printed edition, burning all the copies he could lay his hands on. A revised edition, with all the offensive verses removed and other poems added, became his first published collection, *Poems on Various Occasions*, which Byron called 'miraculously chaste'.[4] A further collection incorporating the earlier ones, *Hours of Idleness*, appeared in June 1807. An unfavourable notice in the *Edinburgh Review* resulted in Byron's first notable satire, *English Bards and Scotch Reviewers*, published in March 1809.

Byron also occupied himself with private theatricals in which he took leading parts, in company with a nearby family, the Pigots. At one point in the summer of 1806 he escaped from his mother's house in the middle of the night after a particularly bad row, and took refuge with the Pigots, who helped him to get to London. Elizabeth Pigot, a sensible girl with whom, for once, Byron did not fall in love, was his especial friend and confidante. Byron left a cornelian heart given him by Edleston in her keeping and told her the details of his infatuations, heterosexual and homosexual, which she seems to have taken with equanimity.

Byron also embarked on a ferocious programme of exercise and dieting, reducing his weight from over fourteen stone to ten stone and a half. His unbalanced diet took a toll: he noted that his hair had lightened in colour from very dark brown to a light chestnut (now known to be a symptom of serious protein deficiency). For the rest of his life he struggled with his tendency to put on weight. Eventually he gave up eating meat and, apart from a little fish, existed mainly on dry biscuits, tea, soda water and potatoes drenched in vinegar. To avoid comment he came to prefer to eat alone. Occasionally he would burst out and gorge himself, and in company he would drink as heavily as any other young man of his generation.

Byron returned to Cambridge for a short visit in June 1807, chiefly to say goodbye to Edleston, who was taking a job in London. Once there he made the snap decision to stay for another year, soon changed to a single term. He was as much trouble to the authorities as ever: forbidden to keep his dogs in college he installed a tame bear – the statutes did not mention bears – in a tower room, and said the bear was to sit for a fellowship. More seriously, he joined the Cambridge Whig club and became part of a circle of clever young men who remained his lifelong cronies and intimates. The closest to him were John Cam Hobhouse, later a Whig Member of Parliament, Scrope Berdmore Davies, a sparkling conversationalist but a compulsive gambler and drinker, Francis Hodgson, who became a clergyman, and Charles Matthews, a brilliant, original young don at King's College.

Byron's powerful personal charm – perhaps an expression of the insecurity that was at other times cloaked in arrogance – attached both men and women to him. His Cambridge friends were genuinely fond of him. They were not fooled, however, by his pose as a romantic outlaw, and reacted to his gloomy outbursts and outrageous pronouncements with affectionate teasing. 'More like silliness than madness' Scrope Davies was heard to murmur when Byron exclaimed, 'I shall go mad!'[5] Throughout his life Byron most valued the people who could make him laugh, easing him out of his black and melodramatic moods by appealing to the sceptical, ironic side of his nature.

Charles Matthews, a companion of Byron's in London as well as Cambridge, was an acknowledged homosexual and seems to have challenged Byron to act out his own desires. Matthews, known as 'the citoyen' because of his daringly radical political views, was, Byron remembered, 'very free in his speculations upon all kinds of subjects', which alarmed the more cautious Hobhouse.[6] Homosexual acts were capital crimes. Even those suspected of homosexuality might have to stand in the pillory and be pelted by the mob, which often amounted to a slow death. If they survived, they served a long prison sentence. Byron's courage was never in question, but he was agonizingly sensitive to public humiliation. If he was to explore his homosexual desires fully it could only be in some country where attitudes were more relaxed. His fixed determination to travel to the East as soon as he came of age had several motives; his actions in Greece and Turkey reveal that sexual curiosity was one of them.

Byron left Cambridge at Christmas 1807, and spent most of the following six months in London. As an unknown scion of a dubious family, with an embarrassing mother, he had no automatic entrée to society, and his guardian Lord Carlisle showed no interest in him. Though gambling was only briefly one of his vices, Byron lived mainly in the company of gamblers, prizefighters such as the famous 'Gentleman' John Jackson, who taught him to box, and prostitutes. For a while he kept two courtesans, one of whom suffered a miscarriage in the hotel where they were living. At last his health, undermined by his excesses and his bouts of dieting, gave way. He boasted that one of them, 'my blue-eyed Caroline, who is only sixteen, has been lately so *charming*' that they were both worn out and ordered to have complete rest.[7] He spent July and August in Brighton, reportedly accompanied by Caroline dressed as a boy and passing as his brother; the cause of more scandal. He wrote little. He was marking time, waiting for Lord Grey's lease of Newstead to expire in September.

As soon as he could take possession Byron went to Newstead, taking Hobhouse with him. The household, headed by old Joe Murray, who had been his great uncle's butler, was augmented by a young page, Robert Rushton, the son of one of the Newstead tenants. Byron was very fond of the boy, who appears with him in a portrait of 1807, and Robert slept in a small room next to Byron's at Newstead in a wing of the house far away from the other servants. Byron also gathered a bevy of young, pretty maidservants, one of whom, Lucy, soon became pregnant by her master.

The estate had been neglected by Lord Grey, and Byron embarked on a lavish programme of improvements. The bills for upholstery alone amounted to over £2,000, even though the magnificent great hall and the chamber above it were left unfurnished and used only for shooting practice and games. The old chapel was turned into a menagerie, where he kept his bear and other assorted animals. Digging in the cloisters in the hope of buried monastic treasure he found nothing but the monks' skeletons, and had one particularly large and well-preserved skull polished and mounted as a drinking-cup — it held more than a bottle of claret. He invited his Cambridge friends for house parties, at which they dressed up in monks' robes (hired from a masquerade warehouse) with Byron as the 'Abbot' of Newstead. The harem of young servant girls also participated in these events, and later accounts of these orgies, almost certainly exaggerated, became part of the Byron legend.

His favourite dog Boatswain died of rabies in November, and Byron, deeply distressed, erected a handsome tomb. It can still be seen in the garden at Newstead, with the epitaph by Byron which ends, to the annoyance of his friends,

To mark a Friend's remains these stones arise;
I never knew but one – and here he lies.[8]

In the will he made on coming of age, besides making provision for Robert Rushton and Lucy and her child, Byron directed that he was to be buried beside his dog, with 'No Burial Service or Clergyman or any Monument or Inscription of any Kind'.[9] This was not a passing whim, for the instruction, against the protests of his solicitor, was repeated in a later will made in 1812.

Byron valued most at Newstead the opportunity for solitude, and the freedom to indulge the eccentric routine he evolved. He never rose before noon, wrote into the small hours and dieted rigorously. The ordinary life of a hunting and shooting country squire was not for him. He was always shy on public occasions, and could not face the official celebrations being prepared by his tenants and servants for his coming of age at the beginning of 1809. He disappeared to London, leaving Hanson, who was already insisting that the sale of Newstead was the only way to square his accounts, as his unsuitable representative. Byron's debts, by his own estimate, now amounted to at least £12,000; an enormous sum in modern terms.

Ambitious to make his mark in public life, as a first step towards a political career Byron took his seat in the House of Lords on 13 March, on the opposition Whig benches. His isolation within English society was cruelly emphasized when he had to enter the House alone, his guardian Lord Carlisle having refused to introduce him.

Byron took his revenge on Carlisle in *English Bards and Scotch Reviewers*, where he described Carlisle's verse as 'paralytic puling'.[10] The poem lashed out in all directions, attacking the famous writers of the day and the reviewers who had rubbished *Hours of Idleness*. A storm of protest greeted this wholesale demolition of the current literary establishment by a young, unknown writer, and Byron later came to regret the poem, and suppressed it.

Restless as ever, Byron now revived his plan to travel abroad, but first he had to find money to fund the journey. Irrationally generous to his friends, hounded by creditors who descended on him as soon as he was responsible for his debts, he was reduced to borrowing over £4,000 from Scrope

Davies, which was not repaid until 1814. But finally, after many delays, Byron and Hobhouse set out from Falmouth on the Lisbon packet on 2 July 1809. With them went Byron's valet, Fletcher, who was to be his faithful companion for the rest of his life, the aged Joe Murray and Robert Rushton.

Letters that Byron wrote Charles Matthews in the carefully coded language they used to refer to homosexual matters suggest that he may have had an ulterior motive for taking Robert abroad with him. From Falmouth he reported that the town was full of 'Hyacinths', i.e. young boys, and that he intended to take one with him. There are references in their correspondence to the 'Abbey' or 'Abbé' Hyacinth – perhaps this one had a connection with (Newstead) Abbey. In a letter of 1811, when Byron was trying to distance himself from his homosexual proclivities, he records his embarrassment over a conversation about adventures with boys and a memory of an unlucky offer of 'two hundred a year' for a 'hyacinth'.[11]

There is no hint of homosexuality, however, in the two characteristically contrasted poems that Byron wrote on leaving England. 'Stanzas to a Lady', a grief-stricken lament, attributes his flight to his loss of Mary Chaworth, whom he had seen at Annesley with her husband and child, and wails:

> . . . I must from this land be gone
> Because I cannot love but one.[12]

The other, 'Lines to Mr. Hodgson', is a ribald verse letter to Francis Hodgson, full of the vigorous enthusiasm of a young man setting out to explore the world. It would be easy, but mistaken, to consider such a contrast a mark of insincerity. Both poems reflected genuine aspects of his complex personality.

THREE

THE ISLES OF GREECE, 1809–11

The isles of Greece, the isles of Greece!
Where burning Sappho loved and sung,[1]

Byron's travels and adventures in Portugal, Spain, the Mediterranean, Greece, Albania and Turkey can be traced in his own incomparable prose and poetry, especially in his letters and in Cantos I and II of his poem *Childe Harold*. Here only some of the most important episodes can be described, from a journey of two years which was of central importance for his development as a poet.

Byron and Hobhouse landed in Lisbon early in July, and travelled on to Spain. Byron preferred Spain to Portugal, and it provided him with the setting for the first canto of *Don Juan*, written nine years later. He sent home Joe Murray and Robert Rushton from Gibraltar; Joe because of his age,

Robert because, Byron confided to his mother, '*boys are not safe* among the Turks'.[2] Byron undertook to pay for his education for three years: 'Let every care be taken of him'.[3] He was still referring to him in letters home a year later. Perhaps because of the parting from Robert, Byron was noticeably depressed on the voyage to Malta, which was reached at the end of August.

In Malta Byron launched into a brief but intense affair with a married woman, Constance Seymour-Smith, referred to as 'Florence' in *Childe Harold*. They talked of elopement, but decided to postpone a decision for a year. It was the first of his many entanglements with married women; apart from a few love poems, it left little mark on him. When they met again as Byron was on his way home, Constance was still eager to fly with him, but absence had, as usual, cooled his enthusiasm.

With his arrival in Greece and Albania the most memorable part of his adventures began, and these countries provided him with landscapes and characters he continued to draw on for his poetry. Travelling was often perilous: they survived a near-shipwreck and a stupendous thunderstorm. Fletcher hated it, missing his wife and family and his English comforts, and Hobhouse, Byron complained, was 'not valiant . . . afraid of robbers and tempests'.[4] Byron revelled in the chances it brought him to escape from the hierarchy of English life, living 'today in a palace, tomorrow in a cowhouse, this day with the Pacha, and the next with a shepherd'.[5]

Greece and Albania were at that time part of the Ottoman Empire, and the classical civilization that Byron was familiar with from his schooldays had been overlaid with the Islamic culture of the Turks. Though Byron was later passionately committed to the cause of Greek independence, he found himself, at first, surprisingly in sympathy with Turkish society, which he found to be courteous, honest and hospitable.

The party travelled up-country to Ioannina, where Byron bought several Albanian costumes, the only expensive items in a part of the world otherwise notable for its low prices. A famous portrait of him wearing one of them was later painted; the costume itself can be seen at Newstead. From there they went through wild and unknown country to meet Ali Pasha, the despotic ruler of Greece and Albania, in the romantic setting of his castle in Tepelene. The mountainous landscape, the feudal system and the mixture of splendour and squalor fascinated Byron. Ali, who had a well-deserved reputation for cruelty and treachery, received him with elaborate courtesy, and Byron, intrigued by his mixture of barbarity and civility, used Ali as the model for several courteous and cruel despots in his poetry. The frank acceptance of boys as legitimate sexual objects pleased Byron – 'In England the vices in fashion are whoring and drinking, in Turkey Sodomy and smoking'.[6] However, this turned a little sour when he realized that Ali regarded *him* as a 'beautiful boy' and a legitimate object of desire. But Ali proved useful in providing letters of introduction and Albanian servants to protect the group on their journey through bandit-infested country to Athens, where they arrived on Christmas Day 1809.

They spent the winter in Athens, learning modern Greek and lodging with a widow, Mrs Macri. She had three daughters, all under fifteen, with whom Byron romped and flirted; the youngest, Theresa, particularly pleased him, and he wrote her a poem, 'Maid of Athens'. But he was less pleased on his return the next year to find that Mrs Macri was 'mad enough' to think he would marry the girl.

In March Byron and Hobhouse left for Constantinople. They sailed first to Smyrna (now Izmir) and thence up the Turkish coast. Byron, with a lieutenant from the ship, repeated the legendary swim of Leander across the Hellespont (the modern Dardanelles) in an hour and 10 minutes, a feat he repeatedly boasted of in his letters. Though it was not the longest swim of his life, there was a fierce current that made it probably the most difficult, and crawl, the stroke now used by all long-distance swimmers, was not known in Europe until long after Byron's death.

At Constantinople Byron found worrying letters. One from Hodgson reported rumours implicating Edleston in charges of 'indecency'. Hanson, from whom he had heard nothing for months, wrote to say that Byron's finances were in an increasingly desperate state. Byron was at last beginning to acknowledge that Newstead would probably have to be sold, and began to think seriously of living abroad permanently. 'England . . . is no country for me', he wrote to Hanson, adding mysteriously, 'Why I say this is best known to myself.'[7]

Byron's worries increased his irritation with his companions; he quarrelled with Fletcher and nearly sent him home. Hobhouse, too, was beginning to get on his nerves, and he was relieved when his friend sailed for home in July. 'I am very glad to be once more alone',[8] Byron acknowledged, though they parted on affectionate terms. Hobhouse later commented that Byron had his own reasons for not wanting an Englishman near him. Certainly it was after they parted that the most actively homosexual phase of Byron's life began.

During his stay in Constantinople Byron became disillusioned with the Turks. Their cruelty and tyranny were increasingly obvious, and when he had seen the sights he soon tired of the city. He returned to Athens in July, and though he continued to travel in Greece, he made Athens his base for the next ten months.

He first returned to his former lodgings with the Macri family, but fled when Mrs Macri offered him Theresa, either in marriage, or for 30,000 piastres. Byron left precipitately on a journey to Patras, going as far as Corinth in the company of the Marquis of Sligo. But Sligo's entourage was too elaborate for Byron's ideas about travel: besides the usual servants it included 'a painter, a captain and a gentleman misinterpreter' whose blunders Byron described to Hobhouse in a long and very funny letter about their misadventures.[9] After parting from Sligo, Byron with his much smaller suite went on to Patras, stopping at Vostitza, where he shot an eaglet, wounding it. In spite of his efforts it died, confirming his distaste for blood sports. He swore never to kill a bird again.

Vostitza was also memorable for Byron's re-encounter with a pretty Greek boy, Eustathios Georgiou, whom he had met in Athens the previous year and who now attached himself to Byron's train. Byron was willing enough at first, but his account of Eustathios, who travelled with him as far as Patras, paints a ludicrous picture of a hysterical and effeminate adolescent, curls hanging down his back, a parasol protecting his delicate complexion from the sun even on horseback. Clearly a relationship of this kind was taken for granted by the Greeks, including the British Vice-Consul, in whose house they stayed at Patras. One wonders what Fletcher made of it. At Tripolitza Eustathios was finally dismissed, Byron unable to bear his sulks and tantrums any longer. 'I think I never in my life took so much pains to please any one, or succeeded so ill',[10] he confessed.

On his return to Athens, Byron found new lodgings in a Capuchin monastery at the foot of the Acropolis, part hotel, part boys' boarding school, and was instantly welcomed by a group of adolescent boys who proved more rewarding. The riotous days and nights romping with Barthelemi, Giuseppe and the rest proved a blissful return to boyhood – or rather a fantasy of what his schooldays might have been. Byron's favourite was the fifteen-year-old half-French, half-Italian Nicolo Giraud, to whom he became very attached. Nicolo, in return, swore that they should live and die together. 'The latter, I hope to avoid, as much of the former as he pleases.'[11] Nicolo gave him Italian lessons, 'sadly interrupted by scamperings and eating fruit and peltings and playings',[12] though Byron did acquire a good knowledge of the language. Aware that this 'vastly happy and childish'[13] interlude was too good to last, Byron took Nicolo with him on several of his excursions in Greece.

The romps in the monastery developed into a full sexual relationship with Nicolo, and possibly with the other boys as well. By October Byron was writing to Hobhouse, in the code the Cambridge set used for homosexual relations, 'tell M[atthews] that

I have obtained above two hundred pl&optCs [the abbreviation used to signify homosexual intercourse] and am almost tired of them'.[14] In November he sent Fletcher home, and employed only local servants, using Nicolo as his go-between and interpreter with them.

Yet this was not an exclusively homosexual period of Byron's life. He also told Hobhouse that he had slept with a number of Greek and Turkish women and caught gonorrhoea from them. There are also conflicting accounts of a tragic adventure which provided the central episode of Byron's 1813 poem *The Giaour*. The 'official' account is given in a letter that Lord Sligo wrote at Byron's request when the poem was published. Byron circulated Sligo's letter widely, after censoring about ten lines. According to this, Byron was returning from bathing at Piraeus one day when he met an execution party on its way to throw a Turkish girl into the sea sewn into a sack, the traditional punishment for a woman found guilty of adultery or fornication. Byron, who knew the girl, bribed the guards to let her go, and smuggled her away to Thebes. But Sligo was not in Athens at the time, and only heard rumours of what had occurred when he returned. Moore, Byron's biographer, gave a more harrowing version in his private journal, closer to the events described in *The Giaour*. He claimed Byron had often told him he knew the girl well, but had believed her to be Greek, not Turkish. She was executed because of his relationship with her, and when he met the party they were carrying her dead body in the sack. This horrific story haunted Byron; perhaps it is the reason for his dark hints to his wife and others that he was a murderer. There are suggestions in his journal for 1813 that the bleaker story is the true one. 'To describe the *feelings* of *that situation* were impossible – it is *icy* even to recollect them.'[15] He was now in a society where relationships with boys were considerably safer than those with women.

By the spring Byron was desperately short of money. The remittances he was expecting from Hanson had not arrived, and he was unable to visit Cairo and Jerusalem, as he had planned. Torn between selling Newstead and remaining abroad permanently, or returning to sort out his affairs, aware that the relationship with Nicolo could not last, he was beginning to be bored with Athens. The euphoric mood of the winter evaporated as spring arrived, and he turned for home.

He took Nicolo with him as far as Malta, where he sent him to school. They never met again, though Nicolo continued to communicate with Byron in affectionate terms, writing from Athens in 1815 to complain that Byron had not answered his letters. But Nicolo represented a side of Byron's life that was best forgotten in England, though at the time of parting Byron was in a mood of deep depression. 'At twenty three the best of life is over and its bitters double', he wrote in his journal. 'My affairs at home and abroad are gloomy enough.'[16] It was not only the parting from Nicolo. He had three illnesses at once: malaria, gonorrhoea and haemorrhoids. He was exchanging an exotic world, a warm climate and a wandering life for money troubles, chills and fogs, and a fixed society in which he felt an outsider.

Byron set foot once more in England on 8 July 1811, after a five-week voyage from Malta. In his baggage, unmentioned and disregarded, were the first two cantos of *Childe Harold's Pilgrimage*, the poem that was to change his life.

FAME, 1811–13

He had that kind of fame
Which sometimes plays the deuce with womankind[1]

Byron lingered in London for nearly a month, in no hurry to return to Newstead. His only contact with the literary world was a minor writer, Robert Dallas, his distant cousin by marriage. He showed Dallas two poems, *The Curse of Minerva*, a biting satire accusing Lord Elgin of stealing the Parthenon marbles, and *Hints from Horace*, an undistinguished 'version' of Horace's *Ars Poetica*. When Dallas asked if he had written anything else, Byron made him a gift of *Childe Harold's Pilgrimage*, telling him he might arrange for its publication if he cared to. Dallas, not noted for his acumen, had the wit to see that the poem was an extraordinary and original production. When one publisher took fright at the unorthodox political and religious views expressed in the poem, Dallas showed it to

John Murray. It was the beginning of a famous and lifelong relationship, which made Murray's fortune and Byron's fame. Future conflict, however, was already foreshadowed; Byron refused to omit some passages Murray considered offensive.

Before the poem was published, Byron was recalled to Newstead by the news of his mother's serious illness. He had to borrow money from Hanson before he could set out, and Catherine Byron had died before he left London. During her two years in charge of Newstead, in failing health, she had done her best to get the estate into order, suffering much from her son's extravagances. After her death it was discovered that she had a collection of valuable jewellery, hoarded through all her money troubles, probably to be handed on to a future daughter-in-law. Byron immediately sold it.

Their relationship had always been stormy, and Byron's letters from abroad were often formal to the point of coldness. Now he sat up by her corpse all night, and was found in tears by her maid. Unable to face her funeral, he remained at Newstead, boxing with Robert Rushton while the service took place. A week later he heard that Charles Matthews had drowned at Cambridge. It was rumoured that he had

committed suicide. His death and that of another
friend, John Wingfield, affected Byron deeply. 'I have
lost her who gave me being, & some of those who
made that Being a blessing', he wrote to Scrope
Davies, begging him to come to Newstead. His
losses induced 'a kind of hysterical merriment,
which I can neither account for, nor conquer'.[2]

Byron made a new will in August, leaving legacies
to his servants. Robert Rushton, now being
educated at Byron's expense, was left £50 a year and
£1,000 when he reached twenty-one. Nicolo
Giraud was to receive the huge sum of £7,000.
There was no mention of Byron's son by his servant
Lucy; probably the child had died. Nor was John
Edleston remembered. Byron had made no attempt
to get in touch with him, and had no intention of
seeing him again, yet when he heard in October that
Edleston, too, had died, while Byron was abroad, he
found himself swamped by acute grief. He felt
ashamed of his emotion, unaccountable to himself
and others. It resulted in a series of emotional
elegiac poems addressed to 'Thyrza'. When these
were published with *Childe Harold* they were
generally supposed (as Byron intended) to be about
a dead girl.

Byron's fascination with homosexuality seems to have been appeased by his indulgences in Greece, and references to such indiscretions, his own or those of others, now made him uneasy. He told William Harness, one of the younger boys to whom he had been attached at Harrow, that he had struggled against and mostly conquered such affections. His feelings for Robert Rushton had subsided into a paternal concern. Now he reinstated his harem of young maidservants at Newstead, sacking the homely middle-aged women employed by his mother. He recalled Lucy, and also employed a local girl, Bessy, and a Welsh beauty, Susan Vaughan: 'all under age and very ornamental'.[3] 'Lucinda to be commander . . . of all the makers and unmakers of beds in the household.'[4]

Jealous quarrels broke out among these girls as they competed for his favours, and the household was soon in chaos. Lucy as former favourite was furious at being ousted by Susan, and Byron, who found himself seriously disturbed by the Welsh girl, had to listen to conflicting tales, in which Robert Rushton was also involved. Susan hinted at a conspiracy, perhaps an affair, between Robert and Lucy; Robert resented Susan's high-handed ways with the rest of the servants, and gave Byron proof of Susan's infidelity, to Byron's chagrin. He treated Susan as seriously as any society lady: 'I do not blame her,' he wrote, 'but my own vanity in fancying that such a thing as I am could ever be beloved.'[5] Byron confessed to Moore that he was suffering from 'ludicrous tribulation'.[6] The seraglio was disbanded and the girls sent back to their families.

Byron returned to London, and to politics. His mother had brought him up as a Whig, and though he was no egalitarian he believed passionately that those in a position of privilege had the duty to care for the interests of the oppressed and powerless in society. Though his political career in England was brief, this was, as he said, the one sphere in which he never changed his opinions. He soon realized that with the Whig party in opposition and his stance too radical for the mainstream, there was little he could do. Yet his maiden speech in the House of Lords, delivered on 27 February 1812, was a carefully prepared, rhetorically brilliant, radical defence of the stocking weavers of Nottingham, which is a model of its kind; it was an exceptional performance for an inexperienced politician of twenty-four.

The introduction of machinery, transforming weaving from a home occupation to a modern factory industry, was causing unemployment and severe distress to the weavers and their families. Riots erupted and the new weaving frames were broken. Rather than seeking to alleviate distress, the Tory government brought in a bill that would impose the death penalty for frame-breaking. Byron pointed out that this was not only inhumane, but ineffective. 'Will you erect a gibbet in every field, and hang men up like scarecrows? . . . Will the famished wretch who has braved your bayonets be appalled by your gibbets? When death is a relief, and the only relief it appears that you will afford him, will he be dragooned into tranquillity?'[7]

Byron's speech had no practical effect, and alarmed his own party more than the Tory government. However, it was reported in the newspapers, and he began to attract public attention. Twelve days later, with the publication of Cantos I and II of *Childe Harold*, he 'awoke to find himself famous'.[8]

Byron had already begun to move in London literary circles, meeting, through the banker-poet Samuel Rogers, such men as the brilliant, alcoholic playwright Richard Brinsley Sheridan, and the Irish poet Thomas Moore. Moore, ten years older than Byron, was the diminutive son of a Dublin grocer. He wrote immensely popular lyric poetry and songs – his *Irish Melodies* are still remembered – which Byron had admired since boyhood. He had an engaging personality and an easy social manner that made him welcome in the salons of London, particularly with patrician Whigs such as Lord and Lady Holland, the circles in which Byron was also beginning to move. Though Byron scoffed, 'TOMMY *loves* a Lord!',[9] he appreciated Moore's genuine affection and loyalty, and after a shaky start they became close if slightly unequal friends. Moore's biography of Byron was necessarily reticent in places, but also perceptive about the contradictions in his character. He wrote of Byron's 'continued struggle between that instinct of genius, which was forever drawing him back into the lonely laboratory of Self, and those impulses of passion, ambition, and vanity, which again turned him off into the crowd'.[10] Moore saw that it was this mixture that gave Byron's poetry its unique quality.

Though Byron enjoyed the company of other writers, he confessed that he felt more at ease with the dandies at Wattier's Club. Though his purse was always open to help authors who fell on hard times, such as Coleridge and the radical journalist Leigh Hunt, whom he visited when he was imprisoned for sedition, he did not see himself as one of them. Perpetually in serious debt himself, Byron still thought it undignified to take money for his publications, instead giving his copyrights away to Dallas and others.

It was of more interest to Byron that *Childe Harold* opened the doors of London's great drawing-rooms. For the next three years he was the most talked about man in London. In spite of his insistence that 'Harold is the child of imagination'[11] he was instantly equated with his hero, as he was with all the subsequent 'Byronic' heroes such as Conrad, Lara and Manfred. This identification was to have a significant effect on his immense popularity and his subsequent downfall. It has continued to influence everything written about him.[12]

The combination of notoriety and physical beauty, with the shyness that could be mistaken for arrogance, made Byron irresistible to women. The many portraits of Byron – he was painted, drawn and sculpted more often than any other writer of the period – give some idea of his looks. He had a rather small head, with Grecian features, a pale complexion, fine eyes and curling auburn hair, worn rather longer than customary. But eye-witnesses agreed that his animation and variety of expression could not be caught by brush or pencil. Sir Walter Scott described his face as like 'a beautiful alabaster vase lighted up by an interior lamp'.[13]

For the first time Byron was besieged by women of his own class. Hanson was pestering him to sell Newstead, and Byron knew that his only hope of keeping his ancestral home was, in the jargon of the day, to marry a 'golden dolly'. He was a most half-hearted fortune-hunter. Instead of finding a wife, he became entangled in one of the most disastrous relationships of his life, with an indiscreet, histrionic married woman.

Lady Caroline Lamb, known as 'Caro', was the wife of William Lamb, who as Lord Melbourne later became Prime Minister to the young Queen Victoria. Noted from childhood for her eccentricity, she was a woman born out of her time, gifted, original and outspoken, but so erratic that she hovered on the edge of insanity. Fair-haired and boyish in appearance, she often dressed as one of her own pages. She was considered too thin to be a great beauty and was not at all the voluptuous dark Mediterranean type of woman Byron preferred. Emotionally she was far too like him for their relationship to prosper. She famously wrote in her journal that he was 'mad – bad – and dangerous to know'[14] – but this was to prove as true of Caro herself.

Lady Caroline first aroused Byron's interest when she refused to be introduced to him at a party – a deliberate ploy, for she had already written him an anonymous letter after reading *Childe Harold*. When they did meet he was attracted by her intelligence and the freedom of her conversation. Caro fell unreservedly and passionately in love with Byron; he, not used to such impulsive and unconventional behaviour in a married woman of his own class, soon became alarmed. Many married women took lovers, but there were rules for such affairs. Caro broke them all. She was extravagantly demonstrative in public; she came to his rooms in Albany unannounced, sometimes disguised as a boy; she showered him with gifts he did not want and tended to give away to other women. She also had a streak of vulgarity he disliked in women. Asked for a lock of her hair, she sent her pubic hair. (Byron was to retaliate later by sending her a lock from the head of his current lover, Lady Oxford, which was the same colour as his own.)

If Byron was not already 'dangerous to know', Caro's behaviour was making him seem more so. Dowagers warned their eligible daughters it was risky even to look directly at his beautiful face. His chances of mending his fortunes by marriage seemed to be rapidly receding, and by May 1812 he was trying to end the affair. 'This delirium of two months must pass away',[15] he insisted. But Caro was not so easy to get rid of, and Byron wavered, hopelessly inconsistent. In August he wrote her a long letter that was intended, he said, to calm her down and reconcile her to a parting, but which reads – and so Caroline read it – as an invitation to renew the relationship. A postscript offered to elope with her, and he signed himself 'ever & even more than ever, Yr. most attached Byron'.[16]

Their turbulent relationship caused both of them much pain, and rumbled on for years, erupting in public scenes, quarrels and reconciliations. It had a

number of consequences for Byron, and one of
these was to change the entire course of his life.
Endeavouring to disentangle himself from Caro, and
feeling that only a rapid marriage would achieve
this, he enlisted the help of the 62-year-old
Lady Melbourne. She was no model of virtue; it was
well known that William Lamb was not Lord
Melbourne's son. But she loathed her erratic
daughter-in-law and became fond of Byron. A
strong and intimate friendship sprang up: many of
Byron's most revealing letters were written to Lady
Melbourne, whom he much admired. 'If she had
been a few years younger, what a fool she would
have made of me . . . and I should have lost a
valuable and most agreeable *friend*'.[17]

Byron had met another young woman related to
Lady Melbourne soon after his first encounter with
Caroline. Annabella Milbanke was her clever, poetic
and mathematically gifted niece. Country-bred and
unworldly, with rigid ideas of morality more
Victorian than Regency, Annabella was the only
child of elderly, doting parents, who encouraged her
to believe herself a genius. Her fortune was modest,
but Byron had finally given in to Hanson's urging
and agreed that Newstead must be sacrificed to pay

his debts. In August a buyer was found, and an advance of £10,000, which paid off some of Byron's more urgent debts, made his need to marry a large fortune seem less acute. Byron had been struck by the simplicity of Annabella's manners: she was a welcome contrast to Caroline, and would, he thought, fit his eighteenth-century concept of marriage as a matter of politeness and mutual convenience rather than love. 'Marriage goes on better with esteem and confidence than romance', he considered.[18] The year before he had joked to his half-sister Augusta that Newstead Abbey was ideal for a married couple: 'my wife and I shall be so happy, one in each wing'.[19]

Increasingly harassed by Caroline, Byron still failed to make a decisive break. Instead, using Lady Melbourne as a go-between, he made a tentative offer to Annabella in October 1812. She turned him down. Her requirements for a husband, relayed in a letter to her aunt and passed on to Byron, were very different from his ideas. Nevertheless, she remained intrigued by Byron and flattered by his attention.

Byron reacted coolly to her rejection. 'I thank you again for your efforts with my Princess of Parallelograms', he wrote to Lady Melbourne. 'Her proceedings are quite rectangular, or rather we are two parallel lines prolonged to infinity . . . but never to meet.'[20] Idling his time away at Cheltenham, he turned for solace to Lady Oxford, whose serial infidelities to her complaisant husband were so notorious that her numerous children, by several different fathers, were known as 'the Harleian Miscellany' – an ironic reference to the early manuscripts collected by her husband's ancestor, Robert Harley, first Earl of Oxford. Jane Oxford was forty, but at the peak of her considerable beauty. Byron was soon deeply and seriously involved with her.

Lady Oxford and Byron suited each other admirably. Byron was to look back on his affair with her, conducted chiefly at Cheltenham and at the Oxford's country seat, Eywood in Herefordshire, with gratitude and nostalgia. He wrote in his journal the following year, at a time of personal disturbance and torment, that Lady Oxford had said to him at Eywood, '"Have we not passed our last month like the gods of Lucretius?" And so we had.'[21] She made few emotional demands on him, but, as a committed Whig and an intimate of the Princess of Wales, Byron knew that she would, if their affair had continued, have shamed him into the political activity he was too indolent to follow through on his own. But there were signs that Byron was again becoming restless, and that the idyll was over. In any event the Oxfords were to leave England in June 1813. Byron seriously considered going with them, telling Caro that she was driving him away by her threats and extravagant behaviour. But neither this, nor alternative schemes of travelling to Persia with Lord Sligo, or to Russia with Hobhouse, were carried through.

Byron, parted from Lady Oxford, and living on tea and bread and butter – one of his periodic diets – was in a sombre mood, reflected in *The Giaour*, published on 5 June. The sale of Newstead had fallen through and his finances were in a perilous state once more. An interview granted at Caroline's insistence, intended by Byron as a final farewell, induced her to behave more wildly than ever. It was at this moment that the arrival of his half-sister Augusta in London, on 26 June 1813, precipitated Byron into an even more dangerous relationship.

SISTER AND WIFE, 1813–16

In him, inexplicably mixed, appeared
Much to be loved and hated, sought and feared[1]

B yron and Augusta, who had not met for four years, were delighted with each other. Byron found that no one understood him like his half-sister. Her easy going tolerance, her unstinting, almost maternal affection suited him far better than the emotional outbursts of Caroline or the moral rectitude of Annabella Milbanke. Talkative, not very clever – Byron's pet name for her, 'Guss', was often changed to 'Goose' – Augusta nevertheless shared his sense of humour, and could laugh him out of his black moods. Though Augusta's financial problems were as acute as Byron's, for the moment everything was set aside but the wholehearted enjoyment of their new relationship, which rapidly developed into sexual passion.

Augusta did not live in Byron's apartments, but they spent almost every waking moment of her three-week visit together. Byron was already the subject of London gossip, and his demonstrative affection for his sister was quickly noticed. It may have prompted Caroline Lamb's last, desperate bid for centre stage. At a party she confronted Byron, who had forbidden her to waltz, and asked him if she might do so now. 'With everybody in turn', he replied. Later she produced a knife, and threatened to stab herself, though she only cut her hand before it was taken from her. The episode was reported in the gossip columns, and the publicity completed Caroline's ostracism from society, though not her ability to take revenge on Byron.

Meanwhile, Byron's infatuation with Augusta continued unabated. He visited her often at Six Mile Bottom, her home near Newmarket, preferably when her husband was away; Augusta made return visits to London to see him. By 5 August Byron was telling Lady Melbourne that his sister was going abroad with him.

Augusta seems to have taken fright at this idea, realizing that she would lose her children and become an outcast. But Byron did not give up the plan to leave England, with or without her. Throughout 1813 he was organizing another tour of the Middle East, and he went on a manic spending spree, running up bills on camping equipment, guns, uniforms to impress the natives and gold items as gifts. He ordered no fewer than six portable telescopes. He also gave Augusta at least £3,000 to pay her husband's debts. The supposed sale of Newstead had made him feel rich, but the purchaser showed no inclination to complete the transaction. Byron could not leave England until Newstead was sold, and in the meantime the estate was left in limbo, the lands neglected and the rents uncollected.

Byron made an attempt to cure his obsession with Augusta in September by his usual method of falling in love with someone else. But after a ludicrous wooing of Lady Frances Webster under her husband's nose at their house and at Newstead, reported in detail to Lady Melbourne, Lady Frances retreated at the last moment, and Byron 'spared' her, telling his confidante, 'I do detest everything which is not perfectly mutual'.[2]

Biographers have disagreed about the extent to which Byron was genuinely affected by Lady Frances

Webster; he even seemed uncertain himself. While he pursued his hostess, he was trying to persuade Augusta to join him at the Webster's house. His passion for her had, he said, 'a mixture of the terrible' which made all other passions insipid.[3] Yet at the same time it was a domestic affection: Augusta was one of the few people with whom he could happily spend time alone. In the snowy January of 1814 he took her to Newstead Abbey. Augusta saw her ancestral home for the first time.

The snow continued to fall, sealing them off from the world. They spent three weeks alone together, during which Byron celebrated his twenty-sixth birthday, reading, talking, laughing. Augusta was pregnant; probably even she was not sure whether the child was her husband's or Byron's.

Though 'Stanzas for Music', which begins:

'I speak not, I trace not, I breathe not thy name
There is grief in the sound, there is guilt in the fame:'[4]

undoubtedly refers to Augusta, in fact Byron could not be discreet, even to protect his much-loved half-sister. Lady Melbourne, his principal confidante, who unfairly blamed Augusta, soon became seriously alarmed and convinced he must marry to save his reputation. Byron also dropped hints to Thomas Moore, with whom he was increasingly intimate. At some point, he almost certainly committed the ultimate betrayal, and folly, of telling Caroline Lamb. He rewrote *The Giaour*, emphasizing the theme of forbidden love, the first in a series of poems dealing with similar subjects. In November 1813 he wrote *The Bride of Abydos*, originally describing the incestuous love of a brother and sister – later changed to that of cousins, to appease his readership. *The Corsair*, which he said was written '*con amore* and much from *existence*',[5] completed and published in February 1814, had a heroine named Medora. Augusta's fourth daughter, born in April, was named Elizabeth Medora. Byron was her godfather.

Byron never acknowledged Medora Leigh, though she herself was later sure she was his daughter. He was fond of all Augusta's children, though it was Georgiana, the eldest, whom he particularly favoured. But he wrote to the shocked Lady Melbourne, soon after Medora's birth, referring to the superstition that the child of incest

must be subhuman. 'Oh! but it is "worth while",
I can't tell you why, and it is *not* an "*Ape*", and if it is,
that must be my fault. . . . You must however allow
that it is utterly impossible I can ever be half so
well-liked elsewhere, and I have been all my life
trying to make someone love me, and never got the
sort that I preferred before.'[6]

Yet, throughout this disturbed and reckless
period, Byron still kept up a regular correspondence
with his 'Princess of Parallelograms'. Though his
analysis of Annabella's character was cool: '[her]
dependence on her own infallibility . . . may lead
her into some egregious blunder', he wrote
prophetically,[7] he was still intrigued by her evident
interest in him and her emotional inaccessibility.
Annabella hinted, quite untruthfully, that she had a
hopeless passion for someone else. Byron was
relieved, rather than disappointed, but he was not
used to rejection, and Annabella still intrigued
him.

Byron's poetry continued to sell in phenomenal
quantities. *The Corsair*, written in ten days, went
into seven editions in the first month after
publication, selling 25,000 copies. Yet Byron
continued to assert that he would write no more –

he began *Lara*, a sequel to *The Corsair*, two months later – and that his work was overrated. Nevertheless, he did for the first time agree to accept payment for his work, taking £700 from Murray for the copyright of *Lara*. He was still giving away large sums of money. A thousand pounds went to his friend Francis Hodgson, to enable him to marry; another thousand was lent to Lady Frances Webster's husband.

The visits to Six Mile Bottom continued, and at the end of July Byron and Augusta escaped to Hastings for a seaside holiday with her children. Augusta, increasingly uneasy, now believed that Byron must marry to save them both. He agreed, without much enthusiasm. Augusta, feeling that Annabella Milbanke was quite unsuited to her brother, favoured her friend Lady Charlotte Leveson Gore. She began negotiations, but Lady Charlotte nervously backed out.

In August the sale of Newstead finally fell through. The purchaser, Mr Claughton, forfeited £25,000 but Byron was so indebted that he now confessed to Moore that he was ruined. Even a moderate fortune seemed attractive, and at the beginning of September he drafted a letter to

Annabella Milbanke from Newstead, where he was staying with Augusta and her children, asking if her objections to him were insuperable. When Augusta, in spite of her misgivings, called it 'a very pretty letter' Byron sent it.

Byron had intended a tentative opening of negotiations, not a proposal. Annabella, however, took it as such, and eagerly accepted, writing twice and enclosing an invitation from her father. When her letter arrived Byron, looking pale and faint, handed it to Augusta, saying, 'It never rains but it pours.'[8]

Byron was now committed. But he was in no hurry to see his new fiancée. Negotiations for a marriage settlement of £60,000, to be paid for by another attempt to sell Newstead, dragged on throughout October, and it was not until the beginning of November that he spent a fortnight at Seaham, Annabella's Durham home. Both on the way there, and on the return journey, he visited Augusta at Six Mile Bottom.

Byron finally left London to get married on Christmas Eve 1814, taking Hobhouse, who was to be his best man, with him. On the way Hobhouse visited Cambridge, while Byron spent Christmas and Boxing Day with Augusta and her family. 'Never was lover less in haste', Hobhouse noted in his diary.[9] They finally arrived at Seaham on the evening of 30 December. The marriage settlements were signed next day, and on 2 January 1815 Byron and Annabella were married at a private ceremony in the drawing-room at Seaham. When Byron had to repeat 'with all my worldly goods I thee endow' he looked at Hobhouse with a quizzical smile. As soon as the ceremony was over Annabella changed into her travelling clothes, and they left immediately for another Milbanke house, Halnaby Hall in Yorkshire. Hobhouse felt, on parting from Byron, 'as if I had buried a friend'.[10]

The couple had known each other chiefly through their letters, and Byron's behaviour once they were alone was not reassuring. According to Annabella he threw himself into a corner of the carriage and only broke his gloomy silence on the wedding journey by shouting a wild Albanian chant. He later told Moore, 'he *had* Lady Byron on the sofa before dinner'[11] – a disconcerting beginning to married life for a young and shy virgin. Then, sensitive about his deformed foot, he told his wife he detested sharing a bed. The following morning, after a night disturbed by nightmares and black depression, he did not get up until noon, and went down to find his wife in tears.

Throughout the two month 'treacle-moon' as Byron called it, savage depression alternated with affectionate closeness, when the clouds lifted and he called her 'Pippin' or 'Pip'. Annabella proved, in spite of her prim upbringing, to be sexually passionate. They read and talked together, and Byron started work on a series of 'Hebrew Melodies' on biblical themes, which pleased Annabella. But he was also writing to Moore inviting him to go to Italy for a year. 'If I take my wife, you can take yours; and if I leave mine, you may do the same.'[12]

Annabella naturally found these changes bewildering. Byron, though he could not keep a secret, had a gift for intimacy that deceived his friends and lovers into believing that each was his privileged confidant, with a unique knowledge of his heart. Throughout his life this led to terrible problems; it was at least in part the reason for Caroline Lamb's refusal to let go of him. It had deceived Annabella into believing, as Byron had encouraged her to do throughout their peculiar courtship, that she would be able to change him. Now, in the grip of the most severe depression of his life, there were times when he took a fierce satisfaction in disillusioning her. Exaggerating his failings, hinting heavily at incest, homosexuality, even murder, he made himself out to be a monster, and intermittently behaved like one.

In March Byron and Annabella spent sixteen days at Six Mile Bottom. Augusta was anxious to make friends with her sister-in-law, and re-establish an affectionate but sisterly relationship with Byron. His behaviour quickly disillusioned her. He made his preference for his sister cruelly obvious, dismissing Annabella to bed every evening and staying up late with Augusta, drinking heavily, while she tried to prevent him. When she refused to resume sexual relations, he turned on her, making coarse remarks to embarrass her and alarm Annabella, comparing intimate details of their physical attributes. Annabella remembered that throughout this torture Augusta was affectionately kind to her, but the relief of both women at parting was heartfelt.

Byron and Annabella moved into 13 Piccadilly Terrace, found for them by Lady Melbourne, at the end of March. Undoubtedly Byron's money worries contributed to his depression, though they could not excuse his behaviour. The Piccadilly house was too expensive, and continued problems over the sale of Newstead, now an urgent priority, drove him half-mad. But in London he had distractions. He busied himself on behalf of Coleridge and Leigh Hunt, urging Murray to publish their work. He met Sir Walter Scott, and they had several long discussions. In spite of political and religious differences the two men liked each other enormously, and admired each other's writing. Scott's reminiscences of Byron are sympathetic and shrewd. Through his friend the banker Douglas Kinnaird, Byron also joined the management committee of the Drury Lane Theatre, and worked hard commissioning and reading plays for the newly re-opened theatre. But his London life was expensive, and Annabella, now pregnant, was unhappy at Byron's intimacy with actors and actresses. She also disliked and distrusted Hobhouse, of whom Byron was seeing a great deal throughout 1815.

Hobhouse, who lived on into the Victorian era, has been portrayed as inhibited, even prudish. In fact he was a man of the world, more anxious for the reputation of a man he sincerely loved and admired than shocked by Byron's behaviour. As early as 1811 he was writing to warn Byron to keep quiet about his homosexual adventures in Greece. Now, alarmed at the state of Byron's mind and finances, Hobhouse was taking an increasing hand in managing his affairs. He devoted himself to sorting out Byron's chaotic financial mess, becoming increasingly suspicious of his lawyer Hanson as he investigated. Hobhouse became convinced that Hanson was corrupt as well as idle, and that the repeated delays in selling Byron's Newstead and Rochdale estates were mostly Hanson's fault. It was Hobhouse who was largely responsible for transferring Byron's business affairs to Douglas Kinnaird, who gradually straightened them out. Byron was not equally loyal to Hobhouse, who felt betrayed when it was Moore, and not he, an older and closer friend, who was entrusted with the memoirs. Already, in April 1814, Byron had given Moore the revealing journal he had kept for the previous six months.

Byron came as close to outright madness during the year of his marriage as he was ever to do. He often threatened violence, to himself and others, and his emotional cruelty to Annabella and Augusta was reported by the servants as well as by Annabella herself in the several statements she made to lawyers. Byron's version of events was lost for ever when his memoirs were burned in John Murray's drawing-room grate, and Annabella's attitude hardened over the years into implacable and self-righteous self-justification, but there is no doubt that during their year of marriage she was confronted with a husband who was out of control and for a while at least impossible to live with.

By November, the bailiffs were in the house. Byron was forced to the painful expedient of selling his library. Annabella, who was eight months pregnant, begged him to go to Seaham with her, but Byron refused to leave London. He had begun an affair with an actress, Susan Boyce, and though he seems to have cared little for her, she was another tool in his torture of Annabella. Annabella was reduced to begging Augusta to stay with them.

Byron had taken to keeping a loaded pistol in his bedroom, and Augusta was afraid he intended to kill himself. He was drinking more than ever. The two women fearfully agreed that he was temporarily insane, and medical advice was sought from

Matthew Baillie, who had seen Byron as a child. Feeling that they needed a man in the house, they asked his cousin George Byron to stay with them, and Annabella also summoned her former governess, Mrs Clermont. On 10 December she gave birth to a daughter, Augusta Ada.

The sight of his child did nothing to change Byron's wild and erratic behaviour. Annabella said that three hours before the birth Byron told her he hoped that both she and the child would die, and when he saw his daughter he said, 'what an implement of torture have I acquired in you!',[13] though at other moments he showed strong affection for her. He was never physically violent to Annabella, but his behaviour so alarmed her attendants that they took to locking him out of her bedroom. On 6 January he wrote her a cold note, asking her 'when you are disposed to leave London' to fix as early a day as possible to go to her parents' house with the child.[14] Annabella left on 15 January; Byron never saw her or his daughter again.

Byron swore that he never intended the separation to be permanent, and that he was shocked when he received a letter from Annabella's father asking him to agree to a legal separation. Two affectionate letters from Annabella, which she claimed she wrote to soothe his insanity, led him to believe that mischief-making by Mrs Clermont and hostility from his parents-in-law had persuaded Annabella not to go back to him, and that she was not to blame. When his letters failed to change her mind, he became determined to oppose a separation in court. However, it became clear that Annabella's lawyers would present evidence that would destroy him and ruin Augusta. Rumours of incest, and the even more serious charge of homosexuality, were already circulating in London – at that time incest, especially with a half-sister, was by far the lesser crime. Public hostility reached the point where Byron's friends began to fear he would be attacked in the streets.

Caroline Lamb, who played a crucial part in spreading the rumours, asked for and was granted an interview with Annabella in March. Caroline told her that Byron had not only confessed to incest with Augusta, but also to having homosexual relations with Robert Rushton and others. Annabella now had quite enough information on which to build a case, and prevent Byron from ever claiming custody of his child.

Whatever Byron was prepared to face on his own account, he could not destroy Augusta. She had a post at Court that brought her a much-needed salary, which she would undoubtedly lose. She had stayed to care for Byron after Annabella left, and though she was writing daily bulletins of his state of mind to her sister-in-law, her presence in the house fuelled the rumours, and society, with the exception of a few brave and loyal friends such as Lady Jersey, turned its back on them both. Byron resigned himself to the inevitable, and began preparations to go abroad.

Even at this traumatic moment he could not resist the distraction of involving himself with a mysterious woman who wrote twice asking for a meeting. She was young, not yet eighteen, intelligent and free-thinking. When she boasted of her connection with Shelley, Byron was intrigued, and allowed himself to be inveigled into bed.

This importunate young woman was Claire Clairmont, stepsister of Mary Godwin, who had gone to Switzerland with Shelley and Mary when they ran away together in 1814, and now lived with them. Claire was rumoured to be Shelley's lover; certainly she shared Shelley's views on free love, and Byron's libertine reputation only encouraged her fascination with him. They had a brief affair, of no importance to him, but Claire, he was later to find, was not so easily shaken off.

By April Byron's somewhat grandiose preparations for departure were completed. He had ordered a huge travelling coach, modelled on Napoleon's, at a cost of £500, and engaged a young doctor, John Polidori, to accompany him. Both were to prove more trouble than they were worth. On 14 April, in great distress, he said goodbye to Augusta. She gave him a Bible that he kept with him for the rest of his life. He paid tribute to her affection and loyalty in several poems. She was 'the solitary star':

> In that deep midnight of the mind,
> And that internal strife of heart,
> When dreading to be deemed too kind,
> The weak despair – the cold depart.[15]

The final Deed of Separation was signed on 21 April, and on the 23rd Byron left London for Dover. Bailiffs immediately entered the house and seized everything. Two days later he left England for ever.

EXILE, 1816–19

Mine were my faults, and mine be their reward.
My whole life was a contest, since the day
That gave me being, gave me that which marred
The gift —[1]

Byron's spirits began to rise as he landed at Ostend – Polidori claimed that he immediately 'fell like a thunderbolt upon the chambermaid'.[2] Travelling always cheered him, though the grandiose coach broke down repeatedly, and Polidori became ill. The consequent delay in Brussels gave Byron the opportunity to visit the battlefield of Waterloo, giving rise to some of the most famous lines in Canto III of *Childe Harold*. By the end of May he had reached Geneva, where he was to remain for four months, renting the Villa Diodati on the shores of Lake Léman.

Walter Scott, on reading Canto III of *Childe Harold*, predicted that Byron's life might end in suicide or insanity. Fortunately, though Byron suffered from intermittent and sometimes severe depression all his life, he had no further episodes of acute psychosis like that of 1815–16. A number of factors kept him afloat. As the disastrous year of marriage receded, he increasingly rationalized and justified his behaviour, and his initial penitence and desire for reconciliation turned to anger at his wife and her supporters. His money problems were less acute on the Continent, where he could live like a gentleman far more cheaply than in England. Also, once cast out by the British aristocracy, he took a more rational attitude to earning money by his writings, accepting £2,000 from Murray for Canto III of *Childe Harold* and the short collection of poems published soon afterwards. As he wrote sardonically in *Don Juan*,

> So, for a good, old-gentlemanly vice,
> I think I must take up with avarice.[3]

Though Byron was humiliated by the public execration in England, and the sense of a forced retreat, exile, for all its bitterness, was also a liberation which was to make possible his greatest poetry. Sales of Canto III of *Childe Harold*, openly autobiographical, were not harmed by the scandal but eagerly bought: 5,000 copies were sold on the day of publication.

Byron had not been long in Geneva when another party of English travellers arrived. Determined to continue her relationship with him, Claire Clairmont had persuaded Shelley and his wife Mary to follow Byron to Switzerland. Byron was not pleased to see Claire, but eager to know Shelley, whose situation had much in common with his own, and they soon became close companions.

Each found much to deplore in the other's attitudes. Shelley was shocked at Byron's aristocratic libertinage, and his treatment of women as playthings, not equals, Byron at Shelley's atheism, revolutionary radicalism and doctrine of free love. Yet there were many points of contact. Shelley, the younger by four years, admired Byron's poetry; Byron, Shelley's knowledge of philosophy and the classics. Shelley even persuaded Byron to read Wordsworth, a poet Byron had always ridiculed.

The Shelley household settled in a cottage near the Villa Diodati. It was a wet, stormy summer, and they all spent time together reading and writing ghost stories. Mary Shelley's, the only story to be finished, developed into her masterpiece, *Frankenstein*. Only Polidori, easily offended, with literary pretensions not matched by any talent, increasingly got on Byron's nerves. Claire was soon visiting Byron on her own, and by April she knew she was pregnant by him. Byron defended himself in a letter to Augusta. 'I was not in love . . . but I could not exactly play the Stoic with a woman, who had scrambled eight hundred miles to unphilosophize me'.[4]

Shelley and Byron bought a boat together, and sailed round Lake Léman, visiting the places associated with Rousseau, Voltaire and Edward Gibbon. They also saw the grim Castle of Chillon. Byron was impressed by Shelley's courage when they were caught in a storm. The slight, pale ascetic, who could not swim, sat with his arms folded, refusing help from Byron and calmly contemplating death.

Byron also renewed his acquaintance with the novelist Mme de Staël, whom he had first met in London. Mme de Staël had been one of the first to suspect Byron's relationship with Augusta, and she now made an attempt to reconcile Byron and his wife. He was willing, but Annabella proved implacable. Byron claimed not to like clever women, but he had an unwilling admiration for Mme de Staël and a lively appreciation of her novels, especially *Corinne*. Also he was grateful for hospitality at her villa at Coppet on Lake Léman. The many English tourists in Geneva had spread scandalous gossip about him, and any rumour, no matter how absurd, was widely believed. To be received by so notable a hostess and introduced to intellectuals such as the German scholar August Schlegel was important to his wounded self-esteem.

In August the Shelleys left for England, taking with them the third canto of *Childe Harold*, *The Prisoner of Chillon*, and the pregnant Claire. Byron had agreed to take responsibility for Claire's child, and promised it should always live either with him or Claire. The Swiss interlude drew to a close. Byron dismissed the tiresome Polidori, and after touring Switzerland with Hobhouse, a journey that inspired the Faustian hero of his dramatic poem *Manfred*, and passionate letters and verses to Augusta, who still filled his thoughts, the two friends left for Italy.

They arrived in Venice in November 1816. It seemed to Byron,

> a fairy city of the heart,
> Rising like water-columns from the sea[5]

It was to be his home for almost three years. He loved the atmosphere of mixed gaiety and gloom; the canals and crumbling palaces; the easy going attitude to sexual irregularities; the gondolas, then all enclosed:

> Just like a coffin clapt in a canoe
> Where none can make out what you say or do.[6]

Byron found lodgings near the Piazza San Marco, and within three days had embarked on an affair with Marianna Segati, the black-eyed young wife of his landlord. Adultery was taken almost as a matter of course in Venice, as long as a woman limited herself to one lover. 'This adventure came very opportunely to console me', he told Augusta, adding that he was at last less tortured than he had been for two years.[7] As English visitors at that time preferred Florence and Rome, there were few to spread gossip about him.

It was while he was in Venice that Byron lost all desire for a reconciliation with Annabella, and though he often suggested he would soon return to England, he became increasingly out of touch with English life and manners. He longed to see Augusta but he was disturbed and puzzled by her letters, full of mysterious troubles. He did not know that she was now under the influence of Annabella, who had embarked on a relentless campaign to force Augusta to confess her sins and repent her love for Byron. Augusta was now showing all his letters, many of them expressing his passionate devotion, to Annabella. Byron's frequent references to visiting England threw her into a panic.

Byron settled into a way of life that alternated solitude and revelry. He had daily lessons in Armenian at a monastery on the island of San Lazzaro, read Voltaire and enjoyed the privileged licence of the Carnival. For exercise he stabled horses on the Lido, so he could ride regularly. He also swam the length of the Grand Canal. His improved spirits were reflected in *Beppo*, rapidly written in the autumn of 1817 in *ottava rima*, the flexible Italian verse form he was to put to even more brilliant use in *Don Juan*. *Beppo*, a light-hearted story of Venetian life and licence, set during the Carnival, is in marked contrast with *Manfred*, with its overwrought romanticism and obvious references to Byron's love for Augusta, and the final, highly autobiographical canto of *Childe Harold*.

During the summer Byron leased a villa at La Mira, on the Brenta canal, and it was here that he met the fiery young baker's wife, Margarita Cogni. 'La Fornarina', as she was nicknamed, was an illiterate Venetian who spoke the local dialect and dressed in the traditional *fazziola* or head-scarf – though she longed for a fashionable hat, to Byron's annoyance. She soon ousted Marianna Segati, but she was only one of many. In Venice Byron plunged into an orgy of sexual licence which shocked those of his friends who were aware of it. He even, in a move reminiscent of his great-uncle's excesses at Newstead, rented a small pavilion where he could entertain his many casual partners, out of the way of Margarita's jealous rages. Shelley was shocked: 'he allows fathers & mothers to bargain with him for their daughters . . . he associates with wretches who seem almost to have lost the gait and physiognomy of man, & who do not scruple to avow practices which are not only not named but I believe seldom even conceived in England'.[8] Byron himself boasted of his exploits, claiming to have had at least 200 women – perhaps more – in 2 years in Venice. He seems to have been determined to avoid any serious relationship, using casual sex as a prophylactic against feeling. Though there is an implication in Shelley's report that these encounters were sometimes homosexual, Byron himself only revealed his adventures with women.

Byron's sense of detachment from England was increased by the news in December 1817 that Newstead Abbey had at last been sold, though the dilatory Hanson did not complete the transaction for nearly a year, and then presented a bill for legal services of over £9,000. Byron settled with him for £5,000, glad to have his affairs arranged at last, and a settlement reached with his creditors. He was tired of being cheated and exploited, and for the last five years of his life he was to gain an undeserved reputation for meanness, often from those who no longer found him an easy touch. However, he never ceased his generosity to those in need, whether ancient Italian peasants, freedom-fighters or fellow writers.

In May 1818 Byron leased one of the four large buildings that make up the Palazzo Mocenigo on the Grand Canal. Here, on the ground floor, there was room for the menagerie he always collected about him. This time it included a wolf. On the floors above there was ample space for servants and guests. Margarita Cogni arrived uninvited, and installed herself as Byron's housekeeper. But she quarrelled incessantly with the other servants, and with him on account of his other affairs, until he eventually dismissed her – upon which she jumped in the Grand Canal, and had to be hauled out by the boatmen. It was an unruly bachelor household, not very suitable for the little girl who soon arrived there.

Byron's daughter by Claire Clairmont had been born in January 1817, and was living at Marlow with her mother and the Shelleys. She was being passed off as the child of a friend, but it was becoming increasingly awkward for the unmarried Claire, much as she loved the child, to keep her daughter with her. In April 1817 Shelley had written to Byron, asking what his plans were for his child, and what he wished her to be called. Byron had been in no hurry to answer, but now that he had a large house of his own in Venice, he was at last ready to receive the two-year-old 'Allegra Biron', as he had decided to name her. 'Desire Shelley to pack it carefully' he wrote to Hobhouse, now back in England.[9]

Allegra arrived with her nurse in May 1818, 'healthy – noisy – and capricious',[10] a partial substitute for the legitimate daughter, Ada, whom Byron could never see. He added a codicil to his will, leaving Allegra £5,000, and decided to bring her up as an Italian and a Catholic, to improve her chances of a good marriage. Though Byron became fond of his child once she was in Venice, he saw little of her, and some of the time she was not even living with him. For long periods he left her in the care of Richard Hoppner, the British Consul-General, and his Swiss wife, who were cold and unloving foster-parents. As he refused to see Claire, or to answer her letters, all communication had to be through Shelley.

Shelley arrived in August to see Byron and check on Allegra's welfare. Byron was not told that Claire, disturbed by letters from Allegra's Swiss nurse, Elise, had come with him. While Claire saw her child at the Hoppners, who told her, with relish, tales of Byron's scandalous way of life, Shelley went to see Byron. He found him lively and happy. Byron was delighted to see him, content to allow Claire access to Allegra (as long as he did not have to see her) and even offered her custody of the child if she wished. Later he retracted this. He believed the gossip that Claire was Shelley's mistress, and did not want Allegra to be brought up in Shelley's free-thinking household. For the moment he offered Shelley the use of his newly rented country house at Este, and Claire had her child with her there for a month. In spite of his disapproval of Byron's way of life, Shelley did not suggest that he was unfit to have charge of Allegra. His ambivalent feelings about his friend are expressed in his great poem of philosophic argument, *Julian and Maddalo*, which was directly inspired by their discussions during this short visit.

Shelley also much admired *Don Juan*, which Byron had begun in July 1818. By September the first canto was finished. It caused consternation among his friends, largely because of the transparent portrait of Annabella as the hero's mother, Donna Inez. He was told it could not possibly be published, and at first agreed. But by April 1819 he had finished Canto II, and insisted that both cantos must be published, without omissions. 'You sha'n't make *Canticles* of my Cantos . . . I will have none of your damned cutting and slashing'.[11] However, he agreed that the poem might be published anonymously. Murray was so nervous of its reception that the two cantos appeared without the name of either author or publisher on the title page. Byron's authorship was instantly recognized, however, and they were fiercely attacked by the critics.

Byron put much of himself into *Don Juan*, without being directly autobiographical, dividing himself between the character of the romantic, impulsive young hero, and the detached, ironic, middle-aged narrator. He had found his ideal form, capacious enough to include his many interests and express the contradictions of his complex personality. He poured into it satire, comedy, romance, pathos and tragedy, moving swiftly and lightly from one mood to another in the pursuit of hypocrisy and cant. As he wrote:

> The new world would be nothing to the old,
> If some Columbus of the moral seas
> Would show mankind their soul's antipodes.[12]

Byron, in his great unfinished masterpiece, came close to achieving it.

At the beginning of April 1819 he also embarked on the last major love affair of his life. Countess Teresa Guiccioli was nineteen, fair-haired and pretty. She had been married, for just a year, to a middle-aged aristocrat from Ravenna, his third wife. Though there were rumours that the Count had arranged the death of one of his previous spouses, and was quite capable of murdering a rival, Byron was alarmed to discover Teresa was as indiscreet as Caroline Lamb. She was, however, more genuine, and soon deeply in love with Byron.

Byron's new attachment to Teresa did not change him overnight. Six weeks after the affair began he wrote a heart-rending letter to Augusta. 'They say absence destroys weak passions – & confirms strong ones – Alas! *mine* for you is the union of all passions & of all affections – Has strengthened itself but will destroy me –.'[13] The following day he wrote Murray a comic account of falling into the Grand Canal on the way to an assignation with the unmarried daughter of a Venetian noble who had been his lover for some months. But at thirty-one he was beginning to feel much older than his years. He was often ill, with fevers and fits of dizziness; his hair was thinning and turning grey; his teeth were loose.

Gradually his commitment to Teresa strengthened. Though his letters to her in Italian are stilted and conventional in their romantic expressions, one letter in English, written in August 1819 in the index of a copy of Mme de Staël's *Corinne*, which he had given Teresa, is touching in its truth of feeling, though it was many years before she knew this. She could not read English, and Byron refused to translate it for her.

Teresa was already pregnant when her affair with Byron began, and, back in Ravenna, she suffered a miscarriage. She begged Byron to come to her, and was so ill that he rushed to her side, and remained in Ravenna. He soon moved into the Count's palace, where their intrigue was carried on under the nose of her husband. 'I can't make *him* out at all', Byron confessed.[14] Alternately complaisant and dangerously suspicious, the Count seemed to be playing a deep game. The lovers were playing a dangerous one, meeting daily while the Count took his siesta. Some of the servants were on their side, others were the Count's spies.

Byron was, for once, out of his depth. Teresa was clearly in love with him, and totally unmercenary. She refused to take money from him, or even expensive presents. But there were moments when he felt she was deceptive, even in collusion with her husband. The Count asked favours, and borrowed money from him, perhaps in return for turning a blind eye. When the Guicciolis moved to Bologna, to another of the Count's houses, Byron followed; after one large loan Guiccioli allowed Teresa to travel to Venice with Byron, ostensibly to consult her doctor. It was an idyllic interlude, the high point of their relationship, and they were on the point of eloping together. For some time Byron had been thinking of joining the revolutionary struggles in South America, and taking Allegra and Teresa with him. At the last moment he drew back.

SEVEN

THE
REVOLUTIONARY,
1819–24

Seek out — less often sought than found —
A soldier's grave, for thee the best;[1]

Byron was growing impatient with the triviality of his life and restless at being in thrall to Teresa. He was also feeling considerable embarrassment at his role as *cavaliere servente*, to a married woman:

> This supernumerary slave, who stays
>   Close to the lady as a part of dress,
> Her word the only law which he obeys.
>   His is no sinecure, as you may guess;
> Coach, servants, gondola, he goes to call
>   And carries fan and tippet, gloves and shawl.[2]

It was a relief when Thomas Moore arrived for a visit. The pleasure of hearing all the London gossip from his old friend turned his thoughts once more to England, and when Count Guiccioli took Teresa back to Ravenna and delivered an ultimatum – she must choose her lover or her husband – he decided to take Allegra to England at the end of November. The journey had to be postponed because he and Allegra were ill; yet when they had both recovered, he found himself on the way to Ravenna, not England.

The early summer of 1820 saw a turning-point in Byron's wavering commitment. In May the lovers were caught by the Count, almost in bed together. A separation became inevitable. Byron could not abandon the woman whose marriage he had destroyed. Divorce was impossible in this Catholic country, but in July the Pope, a personal friend of Teresa's family, granted Teresa a legal separation on condition that she lived with her father.

Byron was also becoming deeply involved in Italian politics. Through Teresa's brother, Pietro Gamba, and her father, both fervent nationalists, he joined the Carbonari, a revolutionary secret society dedicated to setting up a democratic Italian republic to replace the Italian states' Austrian overlords. Byron had always valued the life of action above that of a writer, and this commitment to an ideal that had always engaged his emotions gave a new focus to his life.

Byron plunged into revolutionary preparations. Early in 1821, expecting that an armed struggle was imminent, he decided to put Allegra, now four years old and becoming undisciplined – too much like himself for Byron's comfort – into a convent, much to Claire's distress. The little girl, who now spoke only Italian, was much younger than the other children there, and became a pet of the nuns. But though Shelley saw her there in August, finding her quieter, but not unhappy, Byron never troubled to travel the 17 miles to Bagnacavallo to see his daughter.

The Gamba family was exiled from Ravenna in July, and moved to Florence. Byron remained in the city for a further two months, his movements watched by spies, his letters opened. He was becoming disillusioned by the inefficiency and internal squabbling of the revolutionaries, and when the planned uprising by the Carbonari failed he decided to leave Ravenna.

Shortly before Byron left a fortnight's visit from Shelley improved and deepened their relationship.

Shelley, who had always thought Byron's genius greater than his own, but deplored his morals and behaviour, now found him much improved in every way, due, he thought, to Teresa's influence. Together they hatched a plan to persuade Leigh Hunt to come to Italy and start a new magazine, designed chiefly as a vehicle for their writing, and to provide an income for Hunt. Shelley was now based in Pisa, and Byron decided to join him, with Teresa and her family. Leaving Allegra in the convent and his miscellaneous collection of animals to be disposed of, Byron packed up the rest of his belongings and left Ravenna for Pisa, where he settled into the Palazzo Lanfranchi, the finest house on the Arno. Claire, bound for Florence in the public coach, passed his entourage on the road.

The Shelleys had gathered round them a group of English expatriates, all eager to meet Byron. By the close of 1821 his house had become a meeting place for this Pisan circle. Byron and Shelley were constant companions, playing billiards, engaging in daily shooting contests and spending almost every evening together. Teresa and Mary, in spite of differences of education and outlook, also became friends, and the Shelleys noted with approval Teresa's positive influence on Byron. However, there were tensions; on the subject of Allegra, in particular, Byron and Shelley were at odds. Claire, furious that her child had been abandoned to the nuns, tried unsuccessfully to persuade Shelley to join her in a plot to kidnap Allegra.

In January 1822 Byron's mother-in-law died. Under the terms of his marriage settlement, Byron now inherited a substantial amount of money. But his life was still unsettled. Though he fell in with a boat-building scheme urged on both him and Shelley by the buccaneering fantasist Edward Trelawny, who had just arrived in Pisa, it seemed likely that he would not remain there long. The Gamba family were now regarded as politically dangerous, and the situation was made worse in March when an army sergeant-major was wounded by one of Byron's servants in a brawl in which Shelley was knocked off his horse. Throughout the summer Byron's plans fluctuated between settling in South America, visiting England or going to join the struggle in Greece, where the fight for independence was at a critical stage, with the Turks regaining much of the territory they had lost in 1821.

In April news came from Bagnacavallo that Allegra was ill. Her illness did not at first seem severe, and Byron sent a messenger for more news, but did not go himself. On April 22 Byron heard that she had died two days earlier. The next day he wrote to Shelley, 'I do not know that I have anything to reproach in my conduct, and certainly nothing in my feelings and intentions towards the dead.'[3] But he knew he could have done and felt more for his child. Mary Shelley remarked on his grief and remorse a month later.

In a last, futile act of recognition Byron had Allegra's body embalmed and sent it to England to be buried in Harrow churchyard, where he had sat as a solitary boy. He wrote an inscription for a tablet to be placed inside the church, but because she was illegitimate, the vicar would not allow this. She was buried in an unmarked grave – for years Claire did not know where.

By April the boats commissioned by Shelley and Byron in January were completed. Byron's, named the *Bolivar* after the South American revolutionary, was the larger. It proved an expensive toy, and Byron himself spent little time on it, leaving it mostly to Trelawny. The Shelley household, which now included Edward and Jane Williams, moved to a small house by the seashore near Lerici for the summer, and Shelley and Williams spent every day sailing their smaller boat, the *Don Juan*. In July they sailed to Livorno to meet Leigh Hunt, who finally arrived after many delays to put the plan for the new magazine into operation. Hunt, his wife and six unruly children, moved into the ground floor of Byron's house, where Marianne Hunt immediately found fault with all the arrangements.

A few days later, on 8 July, Shelley, Williams and the boy who acted as crew set off on the return voyage from Livorno to Lerici, in spite of warnings from the local fishermen about the weather. They were inexperienced sailors, and when a storm blew up the frail ship foundered in the Bay of Spezia. All three were drowned. By the time Shelley's body was washed ashore at Viareggio it could only be identified by the copy of Keats's poems in his pocket.

The bodies were buried in quicklime on the beach, as the quarantine regulations required. This did not seem a fitting end for the ethereal and fiery poet. On 16 August, in a ceremony orchestrated by Trelawny, at which Byron and Leigh Hunt were present, Shelley's body was dug up and cremated on a funeral pyre on the beach. Byron, sickened by the sight, swam out to the *Bolivar*, anchored in the bay, to escape it. He suffered severe sunburn in consequence, which made him ill for months. His admiration for Shelley strengthened with his death and his irritation was forgotten. 'You are all brutally mistaken about Shelley who was without exception – the *best* and least selfish man I ever knew', he wrote to Murray.[4]

Through these disasters Byron continued to write prolifically. In addition to a series of tragedies on Italian political themes, and the anti-clerical *Cain*, attacked by the critics for blasphemy, he was constantly adding to *Don Juan*. Murray had only published the first five cantos, and Byron, increasingly dissatisfied with his timorous disinclination to publish anything controversial, and even suspecting him, quite unfairly, of financial crookedness, now intended to let all his new work be published by Leigh Hunt and his brother John.

Byron's acquaintance with Leigh Hunt, begun in 1813, had continued until Byron left England. He was always grateful for Hunt's defence of him when his marriage collapsed, at a time when the rest of the press was implacably hostile. Though he later came to think of him as a vulgarian, it was only after they lived under the same roof that the relationship faltered. Hunt was notorious for financial incompetence, cheerfully living off friends who were expected to keep him and his large family without complaining. Byron and Shelley had financed his move to Italy. Shelley, who had expected to act as the link between the imperious aristocrat and the bourgeois journalist, was dead, but Byron continued to subsidize the Hunts, and to solicit contributions to the *Liberal*, the title chosen by Byron for the new magazine, from his friends. He also tried to help Mary Shelley settle her affairs and get some provision for her from Shelley's father.

Hunt's children were, according to Byron, 'dirtier and more mischievous than Yahoos'[5] and he took to stationing his bulldog on the stairs to stop them getting into his part of the house. Hobhouse, who arrived for a visit in September, strongly disapproved of the association with Hunt and urged Byron not to abandon Murray. However, Byron continued to work for the *Liberal* and *The Vision of Judgement* appeared in the first number. This satire on Southey's eulogy of the recently dead King George III was found so offensive that John Hunt, as the publisher, was briefly jailed and fined for criminal libel.

At the end of September Byron moved to Genoa, in order to stay with Teresa, since the Gambas had been refused permission to remain in Tuscany. He found a house at Albaro, and Mary Shelley and the Hunts shared a house nearby. They continued to work on the *Liberal*, but it finally expired after the fourth number, universally execrated by the critics. It had been an expensive experiment for all involved, but it did provide a platform for Byron's more controversial verse, and John Hunt published Cantos VI to XVI of *Don Juan*, three at a time as Byron completed them, in 1823 and 1824. The poem was not published as a whole until after Byron's death.

During Byron's nine-month stay in Genoa, from October 1822 to July 1823, his involvement with Greek affairs gradually increased. In May he was elected a member of the London Greek Committee, which was raising funds and military supplies for the revolutionaries, and he and Pietro Gamba, in spite of Teresa's protests, prepared to go to Greece to take an active part in the fighting. Byron's enthusiasm was genuine; but it was also a way of escaping the claustrophobia of his relationship with Teresa. He had altered considerably in the past four years. His health, never robust, had been weakened by years of sexual and alcoholic excess, intermittent fasting and recurrent malaria. Hobhouse was shocked by the change in his appearance.

Byron's commitment to Teresa was now firm. Though she was jealous of his frequent contact with Lady Blessington, who visited Genoa in April and May, this was not an intrigue; Byron simply enjoyed reminiscing and gossiping with an Englishwoman. Yet a lifelong relationship with one woman still seemed a sentence rather than a secure haven: the Greek expedition offered at least a temporary reprieve. He had long thought he would die young. Perhaps he would not return from Greece.

Byron was going as agent for the London Greek Committee, but he also poured his own money into the enterprise. He sold the *Bolivar*, hired a brig, the *Hercules*, to take them to Greece, and bought quantities of arms and medical supplies. In addition to these practical measures, he designed and had made, in a last fling of theatrical extravagance, scarlet and gold uniforms and three absurd 'Homeric' helmets for himself, Pietro and Trelawny, who was going with them. Two of them can be seen at Newstead to this day.

They set sail in July, after a painful parting from Teresa. Fletcher, the faithful valet who had been with Byron since his boyhood, his Venetian gondolier Tita and his steward Lega Zambelli, who had joined his household in Ravenna, accompanied him, as did a young doctor, Francesco Bruno. In a curious re-enactment of his early life he took a Newfoundland dog, Lion, he had been given, and later added to his company a young Greek boy, Loukas, who acted as his page. Byron became as attached to the boy as he had been to Robert Rushton, and in the last poems of his life expressed his pain at the boy's indifference to him.

> . . . Love dwells not in our will.
> Nor can I blame thee, though it be my lot
> To strongly, wrongly, vainly love thee still.[6]

Apart from these lyrics, he was to write no more poetry. Instead, the long-wished-for role of a man of action seemed about to begin.

The party reached Cephalonia at the beginning of August. The news was bad. The newly constituted Greek government was weak and divided, the Turks strong. For the time being Byron remained on board the *Hercules*, in the harbour of Argostoli, and then in a small house at Metaxata, waiting for developments. He was besieged by every faction for money, help and support, and he wanted to see where he could be of most use before making a move. Byron was under no illusions about the Greeks, but he understood them better than many of the other English Philhellines. He knew many of them were thieves and liars and that their atrocities were equal to those of the Turks, and he knew why. 'The Greeks have been downright Slaves for five centuries, and there is no tyrant like a Slave!'[7]

The town of Missolonghi, a key port on the mainland of western Greece, became the head-quarters of Prince Mavrocordatos, the first President of Greece, in December. It was under siege by the Turks, and Byron decided that this was where he could be most useful. He agreed to maintain a band of 500 Suliotes, fierce Albanian tribesmen, for a year. Trelawny had already departed to join a Greek bandit in Attica, but the rest of Byron's party, augmented by another doctor, Julius Millingen, and the page Loukas, set sail with him. After a hazardous journey, during which they narrowly evaded an attack by the Turkish fleet and were nearly shipwrecked, he disembarked at Missolonghi on 5 January 1824, to an enthusiastic welcome.

Missolonghi was a dreary town built on a malarial marsh, and the house in which Byron lodged, though one of the best in the town, was cramped and inadequate. He bore the discomfort without complaint, but it soon became clear that the Greeks were as faction-ridden and incompetent as the Carbonari had been. What they wanted from Byron was not personal heroism but money, and he found he was being cheated on all sides. Angry and distressed, in mid-February he suffered what appeared to be an epileptic fit.

Though he recovered in a few days, Byron remained weak and depressed, with fits of giddiness and irrational feelings of nervousness. He was saddened by the cruelty of the Greeks to captured Turks, and managed to rescue a Turkish mother and daughter from slavery. He thought of adopting the little girl and sending her to England as a companion for Ada, but finally sent her to safety in Cephalonia with her mother.

As spring came, bad weather prevented Byron from taking his usual daily rides, and he became increasingly restless. On 9 April he insisted on going out and was caught in a storm. That night he was feverish, with rheumatic pains, but rode again the next day. By 13 April he was seriously ill, and intermittently delirious. The doctors wanted to bleed him, which he strenuously resisted. Without Byron in charge, there was, according to one of the most reliable witnesses to his last days 'neither method, order, nor quiet, in his apartments'.[8] Increasingly weak, he finally gave in to the doctors, and was repeatedly bled and purged. In his weakened state this almost certainly hastened his death, if it did not cause it. On Easter Sunday, 18 April, it was clear he was dying. He made incoherent attempts to convey his last messages to Fletcher, before lapsing into unconsciousness. He died at six in the evening the following day. General mourning was ordered throughout Greece, and the usual Easter celebrations were cancelled.

In one of his last coherent requests Byron had insisted 'Let not my body be hacked, or be sent to England. Here let my bones moulder. Lay me in the first corner without pomp or nonsense.'[9] But those around him thought they knew better. After a crude autopsy, the body was embalmed and returned to

England, where it arrived on 2 July. Hobhouse, the last person to bid farewell to Byron when he left England in 1816, was the first on board the boat bringing him home.

Since the Dean refused permission for Byron to be buried in Westminster Abbey, he was buried in the family vault at Hucknall Torkard, near Newstead, with his mother and his great-uncle, the 5th Baron. 'He was buried like a nobleman – since we could not bury him as a poet', wrote Hobhouse.[10] The solemn funeral procession took four days to make the journey from London: silent crowds lined the roads all the way along the route.

NOTES

The following abbreviations have been used in the notes:

L & J: *Byron's Letters and Journals*, ed. Leslie A. Marchand, 13 vols, John Murray, London 1973–94

Notices: Thomas Moore, *Letters and Journals of Lord Byron, with Notices of his Life*, 2 vols, John Murray, London, 1830

Portrait: Leslie A. Marchand, *Byron: A Portrait*, Pimlico, London, 1993

Quotations from Byron's poems are given with their date of first publication, or, if posthumously published, with the date of composition.

INTRODUCTION

1. *Don Juan*, Canto III, verse 88, 1821.

2. Leslie A. Marchand, *Byron: A Biography*, 3 vols, London, John Murray, 1957, Vol. 3, p. 1249.

3. Peter Quennell (ed.), *The Journal of Thomas Moore 1818–1841*, London, Batsford, 1964, p. 95.

CHAPTER ONE

1. 'I would I were a careless child', 1808.

2. *The Deformed Transformed*, 1824.

3. *Don Juan*, Canto XVII, verse 1, 1823.

4. *L & J*, 3, pp. 221–2.

5. *Portrait*, p. 22.

6. C. J. Tyerman, 'Byron's Harrow' in *Byron: The Harrow Collection*, Harrow, privately printed, 1994, p. 27.

7. *Idem*.

8. *Notices*, Vol. 1, p. 177.

9. *Portrait*, p. 21.

10. Louis Crompton, *Byron and Greek Love*, London, Faber & Faber, 1985, p. 108.

11. 'Childish Recollections', 1807.
12. *L & J*, 1, p. 45.
13. *Idem*, p. 57.
14. *L & J*, 4, p. 112.
15. *L & J*, 9, p. 37.

CHAPTER TWO

1. *Don Juan*, Canto I, verse 212.
2. *L & J*, 5, p. 169.
3. *L & J*, 3, p. 225.
4. *L & J*, 1, p. 103.
5. T.A.J. Burnett, *The Rise and Fall of a Regency Dandy: The Life and Times of Scrope Berdmore Davies*, Oxford University Press, 1983, p. 33.
6. *L & J*, 7, p. 234.
7. *L & J*, 1, p. 157.
8. 'Inscription on the Monument of a Newfoundland Dog', 1809.
9. *L & J*, 1, p. 202.
10. *English Bards and Scotch Reviewers*, l. 725, 1809.
11. *L & J*, 2, p. 124.
12. 'Stanzas to a Lady, on Leaving England', 1809.

CHAPTER THREE

1. *Don Juan*, Canto III, verse 86.
2. *L & J*, 1, pp. 221–2.
3. *Idem*, p. 222.
4. *Idem*, p. 231.
5. *L & J*, 2, p. 9.
6. *L & J*, 1, p. 238.
7. *Idem*, p. 232.
8. *L & J*, 2, p. 9.
9. *Idem*, p. 5.
10. *Idem*, p. 6.
11. *Idem*, p. 12.
12. *Idem*, p. 13.
13. *Ibid*.

14. *L & J*, 2, p. 23.
15. *L & J*, 3, p. 230.
16. *L & J*, 2, p. 65.

CHAPTER FOUR

1. *Don Juan*, Canto XV, verse 57.

2. *L & J*, 2, p. 69.

3. *Idem*, p. 131.

4. *Idem*, p. 106.

5. *Idem*, p. 159.

6. *Ibid*.

7. Andrew Nicholson (ed.), *Lord Byron: The Complete Miscellaneous Prose*, Oxford, Clarendon Press, 1991, p. 26.

8. *Portrait*, p. 116.

9. *Idem*, p. 385.

10. *Notices*, Vol. 1, p. 592.

11. Preface to *Childe Harold*, 1812.

12. Andrew Elfenbein, *Byron and the Victorians*, Cambridge University Press, 1995, Chapter 1, 'Byron and the Secret Self' has an excellent discussion of this point.

13. Norman Page, *Byron: Interviews and Recollections*, London, Macmillan, p. 76.

14. *Portrait*, p. 118.

15. *L & J*, 2, p. 177.

16. *Idem*, p. 185.

17. *L & J*, 3, p. 219.

18. *L & J*, 2, p. 199.

19. *Idem*, p. 86.

20. *Idem*, p. 231.

21. *L & J*, 3, p. 210.

CHAPTER FIVE

1. *Lara*, Canto I, verse 17, 1814.

2. *L & J*, 3, p. 151.

3. *L & J*, 4, p. 23.

4. 'Stanzas for Music', 1814.

5. *L & J*, 3, p. 243.
6. *L & J*, 4, p. 104.
7. *L & J*, 3, p. 108.
8. *Portrait*, p. 176.
9. *Idem*, p. 187.
10. *Idem*, p. 188.
11. *Idem*, p. 191.
12. *L & J*, 4, p. 269.
13. *Portrait*, p. 209.
14. *L & J*, 5, p. 15.
15. 'Stanzas to Augusta', 1816.

CHAPTER SIX

1. 'Epistle to Augusta', verse 4, 1816.
2. *Portrait*, p. 236.
3. *Don Juan*, Canto I, verse 216.
4. *L & J*, 5, p. 92.
5. *Childe Harold*, Canto IV, verse 18, 1818.
6. *Beppo*, verse 19, 1817.
7. *L & J*, 5, p. 141.
8. F.L. Jones (ed.), *The Letters of Percy Bysshe Shelley*, 2 vols, Oxford University Press, 1964, Vol. 2, p. 58.
9. *L & J*, 6, p. 25.
10. *Idem*, p. 39.
11. *Idem*, p. 105.
12. *Don Juan*, Canto XIV, verse 101.
13. *L & J*, 6, p. 130.
14. *Idem*, p. 163.

CHAPTER SEVEN

1. 'On this day I complete my thirty-sixth year', 1824.
2. *Beppo*, verse 40.
3. *L & J*, 9, p. 147.
4. *Idem*, pp. 189–90.
5. *L & J*, 10, p. 11.
6. 'Love and Death', 1824.

7. 'The Present State of Greece' in A. Nicholson (ed.), *Lord Byron: The Complete Miscellaneous Prose*, Oxford, Clarendon Press, 1991.

8. William Parry, *The Last Days of Lord Byron*, London, Knight and Lacey, 1825.

9. *Portrait*, p. 457.

10. *Idem*, p. 470.

BIBLIOGRAPHY

PRIMARY SOURCES

McGann, J. (ed.). *Lord Byron: The Complete Poetical Works*, 7 vols, Oxford, Clarendon Press, 1980–93

Marchand, L.A. *Byron's Letters and Journals*, 13 vols, London, John Murray, 1973–94

Nicholson, A. (ed.). *Lord Byron: The Complete Miscellaneous Prose*, Oxford, Clarendon Press, 1991

SECONDARY SOURCES

Blessington, Lady. *Conversations of Lord Byron*, ed. E.J. Lovell, New Jersey, Princeton University Press, 1969

Boyes, M. *My Amiable Mama: The Biography of Mrs Catherine Gordon Byron*, privately printed, *c.* 1991

Burnett, T.A.J. *The Rise and Fall of a Regency Dandy: The Life and Times of Scrope Berdmore Davies*, Oxford University Press, 1983

Crampton, L. *Byron and Greek Love: Homophobia in 19th Century England*, London, Faber & Faber, 1985

Elwin, M. *Lord Byron's Wife*, London, John Murray, 1974

——. *Lord Byron's Family, Annabella, Ada and Augusta 1816–1824*, London, John Murray, 1975

Foot, M. *The Politics of Paradise: a Vindication of Byron*, London, Collins, 1988

Gittings, R. and Manton, J. *Claire Clairmont and the Shelleys*, Oxford University Press, 1992

Bibliography

Graham, P.W. *Lord Byron's Bulldog: The Letters of John Cam Hobhouse to Lord Byron*, Columbus, Ohio, Ohio State University Press, 1984

Gunn, P. *My Dearest Augusta: a Biography of the Honourable Augusta Leigh*, London, The Bodley Head, 1968

Holmes, R. *Shelley: the Pursuit*, London, HarperCollins, 1994

Lamb, Lady C. *Glenarvon*, London, Everyman Dent, 1995

Marchand, L.A. *Byron: A Biography*, 3 vols, London, John Murray, 1957

———. *Byron: A Portrait*, London, Pimlico, 1993

Marshall, W.H. *Byron, Shelley, Hunt and the Liberal*, Oxford University Press, 1960

Moore, D.L. *The Late Lord Byron*, London, John Murray, 1961

———. *Lord Byron: Accounts Rendered*, London, John Murray, 1974

Moore, T. *Letters and Journals of Lord Byron: with Notices of his Life*, 2 vols, London, John Murray, 1830

Nicholson, H. *Byron: The Last Journey*, London, Prion Books, 1999

Origo, I. *Byron: The Last Attachment*, London, John Murray, 1949

Page, N. (ed.). *Byron: Interviews and Recollections*, London, Macmillan, 1985

Quennell, P. *The Journal of Thomas Moore*, London, Batsford, 1964

Robinson, Charles E. (ed.). *Lord Byron and his Contemporaries: Essays from the Sixth International Byron Seminar*, Newark and London, University of Delaware Press, 1982

Bibliography

Rutherford, Andrew (ed.). *Byron: the Critical Heritage*, London, Routledge & Kegan Paul, 1970

Trueblood, P.G. *Byron's Political and Cultural Influence in Nineteenth Century Europe*, London, Macmillan, 1981

Tyerman, C.J. 'Byron's Harrow', in *Byron: The Harrow Collection*, Harrow, privately printed, 1994

Vassallo, Peter. *Byron: the Italian Literary Influence*, London, Macmillan, 1984

White, Terence de Vere. *Tom Moore: the Irish Poet*, London, Hamish Hamilton, 1977